# Taking

## of

# *Angels*

# *Unaware*

## By

## AMY BUGGLE

ISBN 978-1-0980-6699-4 (paperback)
ISBN 978-1-0980-7001-4 (hardcover)
ISBN 978-1-0980-6700-7 (digital)

Christian Faith Publishing, Inc.
832 Park Avenue
Meadville, PA 16335
www.christianfaithpublishing.com

Printed in the United States of America

To all the DLC families, parents and children,
who will always be my heroes.

*Do not forget to entertain strangers, for by so doing some have unwittingly entertained angels.*

—Hebrews 13:2 (NKJV)

*John Wesley explained this verse by saying, "A guest may be worth more than he appears and may have angels attending him, though unseen."*

# TABLE OF CONTENTS

# CHAPTER 1

# *God Influences Even Children*

*Train up a child in the way he should go; even when he is old he will not depart from it.*

—Proverbs 22:6

The first time I saw a child with cerebral palsy, it was on an educational video at a day of training for youth volunteers. The child I remember in the video was struggling to sit up on his own; his legs spread abnormally apart, and his arms were waving uncontrollably, but he was smiling this beautiful smile that was quite contagious. His joy was evident, and something about him made me feel joyous and made me want to help keep his joy alive. I was ten going on eleven and remember thinking I can't wait until I'm old enough to volunteer too. The "Volunteens" my mom was supervising—herself a volunteer at the Hope Haven Children's Hospital—had to be, at least, twelve.

I would not have to wait very long. The United Cerebral Palsy director assumed I was already twelve and asked me when I could start. I was tall for my age and always looked older than I really was. I admitted I wasn't old enough, and she said, "You look old enough to me, if you want to give it a try." This made me feel quite grown up and quite important. This boost to my ego at such a young impressionable age was just what I needed to get me sold on the idea of helping children with special needs. She didn't have to ask me twice; of course, I wanted to give it a try and started the next day as a real "Volunteen" helping young children with cerebral palsy and other physical challenges, with their swimming therapy.

I had never done anything like this before. I had, however, been introduced to the world of "special-needs kids" within my own family. The third daughter of my Aunt Alice, my mother's youngest sister, and my Uncle Johnny had been born on June 5, 1964, with Down syndrome and a heart defect that had taken her life at the age of four. She was born the same year and within three weeks of my younger brother, Marc. I had heard all about Tina, mostly through stories told about her as I was too young to remember much.

Aunt Alice was shocked by doctors who told her that her new baby was "mongoloid" and tried, immediately, to get her to sign papers, giving them permission to take Tina and put her in an institution. She was told this news without Uncle Johnny, or any other family member, even being there. Though shocked and scared, she refused to sign. She held her resolve and, with tears flowing, demanded to wait for her husband to arrive. When Johnny arrived, he was in full agreement, and they gave each other the courage and strength to stand their ground and refuse to let the doctors take Tina. This was their beautiful little girl! Neither one of them even knew what the term "mongoloid" meant. They had never heard of it and didn't believe the doctors, at first. Once the doctors showed them the signs—the slanted eyes with folded eyelid, her short fingers, and the floppy muscles—they understood and finally did believe what the doctors were telling them.

In Tina's case, as in many children with Down syndrome, she had a severe abnormality in her heart. The doctors also revealed that Tina would have slower-than-average development and cognitive impairment as an adult. This, however, did nothing to change their minds about keeping Tina. The doctors even told them that Tina would be a burden to the whole family, and it wouldn't be fair to her other two children to bring Tina home. I guess what was fair to Tina didn't matter back then.

I was amazed thinking about how hard it must have been for them to push back against the doctors demands. I later asked Aunt Alice what made her feel that strongly about keeping Tina with the doctors urging her to give her up. Back then, doctors were seen as highly educated and such authority figures. Alice told me, "She was my baby, what do you think my mother would have said if I had given her away just because she was flawed?" She may have been more afraid of her mother's disapproval than she was of the doctors. I still see it as extremely brave for the time. Most young women would have caved in under that kind of pressure.

Her mother, my Gran, did love Tina as much, if not more than her other fourteen grandchildren. All of the family supported their decision to keep little Tina and helped take care of her. She was never a burden to her two older sisters, Tammie and Tracy, and brought so much joy to the household. They treated her just like their other two daughters and said she was learning and very smart. Aunt Alice says they never regretted the decision to take Tina home that day. I'm not sure where their resolve to keep Tina and treat her just like the other girls came from, especially in the '60s, but I do believe it had a big influence on me and my beliefs about children that are born with handicapping conditions. This was obviously the way everyone in my family believed, and it is a great legacy to have been passed down to me. All children are equally valuable and are to be treasured!

At the time, heart surgery had not advanced to the point that it was commonly done for children. I am not sure if the doctors even knew she had a large hole in her heart, and if they did, not much could be done about it. As Tina grew, her heart could not keep up with her size. One day, at breakfast, her little damaged heart could no longer pump the blood well enough to keep up her oxygen levels. My aunt and uncle had no idea what was happening and why she was struggling for air. No one had warned them that something like this could happen. She was placed under an oxygen tent, but that was only a temporary measure, and nothing more could be done. This was a devastating loss for them, and the whole family was shocked and saddened by Tina's sudden illness and death. I was only six at the time, but this must have subconsciously influenced me and the empathy I have for families of children with special needs.

For many years, I held a grudge with the doctors for not doing more. I always wondered if her disability was the reason heart surgery was not an option but have since learned that doctors were not trained to do such a risky surgery on a child. Today, the surgery that could have saved her life is fairly common, and most children with Down syndrome go on to live well into adulthood and live very healthy lives. But Tina left an indelible mark on all of us in the family. Her sweet, spunky personality is still remembered by all of us today, and I know her life influenced mine for the better.

In honor of Tina, my family became involved with fund-raising for Pine Castle, a program for adults with intellectual and developmental disabilities. Pine Castle is still a thriving program in Jacksonville, Florida, today. I remember helping with a yard sale benefiting the program and collecting items from home to donate. I think this was the beginning of God's preparation for the task He would set before me.

> To everything there is a season, a time for every purpose under heaven: A time to plant, and a time to pluck what is planted. (Ecclesiastes 3:1–2b)

> As you do not know the way of the wind, or how the bones grow in the womb of her who is with child, so you do not know the works of God who makes everything. In the morning you sew your seed for you do not know which will prosper, either this or that. (Ecclesiastes 11:5–6)

So one thing led to another, and I ended up volunteering with children that had special needs at the United Cerebral Palsy program. My mother's compassion for children in need because of the love of her sister after the loss of a child led me to do the same. Looking back, I can see all the connections, but I couldn't see it then. All I knew is that I loved being with those kids, and I loved learning creative ways to help them accomplish new things, especially things that doctors had told their parents they would never accomplish. That seemed to happen often. I know doctors need to prepare parents for the negatives that may happen with children that have challenges, but they forget, sometimes, the joys of having a child with developmental delays. It makes the victories the children have in life even sweeter.

My first experience volunteering was with the swimming-therapy program that United Cerebral Palsy offered over the summer months. It was amazing for me to see a child that couldn't walk get in the pool and learn to swim. So many creative things could be taught to children with disabilities in the water, and their motivation was always high because they loved the water and how it transformed them. Somehow, in the water, they were like every other kid, and while they were swimming, they were learning breath control and would get excited and start to talk, even if they hadn't before. I remember one little blond-headed girl with spina bifida. She was sitting on the side of the pool with her feet dangling in the water. I started a conversation with her and asked if the water in the pool felt cold. She answered matter-of-factly, "I don't know, I have no feeling in my legs." I was so embarrassed that I hadn't thought about that but, then, became enamored with her courage to be getting in water without the use of her legs.

Every day, the children would amaze me with their courage, and that is still true today. Things that would knock the average adult down and destroy many of us if we were in a similar circumstance is just the way life is to them. They make even adults feel foolish about the things that worry us. Our worries and fears pale in comparison to the things they endure. The inspiration these kids give the world is just limitless. I loved being around that and still do.

> For it is written, I will destroy the wisdom of the wise, and will bring to nothing the understanding of the prudent. (1 Corinthians 1:19)

Miracles were happening all around me on a daily basis, and I was part of the miracle. What could be more fun than that? I became addicted to this work and these kids and loved every part of the job. From swim lessons, to helping in the preschool classrooms, to helping the kids feed themselves at lunchtime, to changing diapers; these were all ways to help the children to learn and get better and to just keep them full of that joy. It kept me full of joy too.

Every summer, for the rest of my teenage years, this was how I spent my summer vacation. The first day of summer break until the last day of summer break, I was assisting the teachers at United Cerebral Palsy. Funny that people see this as a sacrifice of my summer, but I saw it as a gift to be with these little angels that looked up to me. They made each summer day exciting and fun.

Each time I returned, however, it felt a little strange at first. I wouldn't know the kids or how to handle them or how to communicate with them. I would think to myself, "Did I really do this last year?" The kids all looked much more disabled than I remembered, but as soon as I got to know them as individuals—as little people again—that fear would melt away, and I would just see those precious children for who they were. They really are just beautiful children that have been given some really tough breaks and can overcome the obstacles they have been given with the right opportunities. Each of us is just as special to God and just as important, each of us with unique problems and qualities. Some of our challenges are much less obvious, some of which we are aware and some not.

> But from those who seemed something, whatever they were, it makes no difference to me. God shows personal favoritism to no man—for those who seemed to be something added nothing to me. (Galatians 2:6)

> See what kind of love that the Father has given to us that we should be called the children of God; and so we are. (1 John 3:1)

This hands-on education I received from the United Cerebral Palsy program was invaluable. I learned how to handle the children safely, how to pick them up and carry them, how to talk to them and with them. Most importantly, I learned that talking isn't always with words. Many of the children couldn't speak, but once you paid attention, they could communicate to you in their own way. It might be by asking them Yes-or-No questions and waiting for the head nod accordingly. It might be by an eye blink; one for "no" or two for "yes." It might be a certain vocalization that you could understand once you learned the specific sound. More often than not, it was just an expression. A facial grimace or frown was a negative and letting you know that was not what they wanted. The big smile and open mouth with happy eyes meant you were on the right track and that you had found what they were trying to tell you. At lunch or snack time, choices could be held up, and the child would look at the drink they wanted or at the cookie or so on. It was a whole new language that wasn't impossible to decipher; you simply had to slow down the pace and wait for a response. Paying attention for the subtle cues was the answer to communicating. This is a lesson we all could use in life with all people.

During the time of swimming lessons, I even learned how to dress them, and for children with tight muscles and other disabilities, this can be quite a challenge. It was always tricky to get the arm in the hole of a shirt if a child's arm won't bend. Many of the children wore splints and braces. Back at this time, the braces were complex contraptions with metal bars and clasps and leather strapping. They would lock into place at the knees for support in standing, and then, you had to remember to unlock them for the children to bend at the knee to sit. The braces Forrest Gump wore are a perfect visual example. And they weighed about five pounds each, making each child much heavier to carry.

Many of the children needed wheelchairs as well, and the wheelchairs were each custom built. This meant they all were a little different to use. Each had special strappings and trays and locks so the children wouldn't roll unexpectedly. The chairs had to be locked before placing a child in them, or they could roll away as you put them in the seat. This is one thing I learned the hard way. The children had to be strapped at the waist and, sometimes, the chest, and there were supports for the head, as well, for some children. The strap at their waist was very important. If it was too loose, a child could slip under it and fall out of the seat if they wiggled or had poor trunk control and weak tummy muscles. And if a child had tight muscles, they could pop the strap off by extending their bodies upward. When they got excited, the muscles would tighten extra hard, and they could almost pop straight up out of the seat. Each tray slid on and locked on the front of the chair differently too. Trial and error are a tough way to learn but, maybe, the best way. Many times, if I was struggling, the children themselves would come to my aid and tell me what to do. They all had such patience with me and were just appreciative of the attention they were getting from someone new.

The child development center of United Cerebral Palsy became like a second home to me. It changed drastically over the years. From the swimming lessons in a pool, to classrooms set up in the auditorium of Hope Haven Hospital, to a wing in the hospital. It, then, moved to the Unitarian Church in some rooms we shared with the church. I followed them everywhere. Even to a house on the other side of town. I had never been to the west side of Jacksonville and was so scared to travel over the bridge at sixteen years old. But I ventured there, in spite of my fears, to be with the kids and help out that summer. I now live on that side of town, ironically, very near the little house that was home to the preschool where I was so terrified to travel. It is still a preschool of some kind, and I hardly recognized it when I discovered it.

Each place holds memories for me, all fond. These places were where the dream started to create a school of my own. This is also where I modeled much of my school programming and current classroom setups. These places all had different staff but the same theme of giving children the opportunity to learn and develop and give the families a place of hope and support.

We did circle time with the children in the morning, did art and fun, creative activities with them, therapy time, and lots of stimulation. I remember the teachers never did enough, in my opinion, and I would always add in extra learning opportunities to the routine. Even diaper-changing time became a learning game.

I would call out each child's name, and when they looked, I would toss them their diaper to catch. This was teaching them to respond to their name and use fine motor skills. I would get them to help with undressing and dressing themselves rather than doing it for them. If we were working on potty training, I could add in some speech-therapy time while they sat on the toilet. We worked on naming the food they were eating at lunchtime, naming the color of the food, and I would let them feed themselves, even if it meant a big mess. And I cleaned plenty of messes up afterward. Sometimes, there was more food on the floor than in their bellies, but they were doing it themselves, and that was what was important.

It was easy for me to spot the children that had "hidden" intelligence. I remember thinking that the teachers didn't see it most of the time. The ones that followed me with their eyes and had facial responses that were appropriate were obviously smarter. Especially the ones with a sense of humor. If I could make them laugh at the jokes and funny things I did, that was a big clue. Some of the most physically delayed were not seen as very bright, but I knew this wasn't the case. I would work to expose their intelligence in different ways, and many times, the teachers would catch on. I wasn't smarter about it, just in tune. Maybe, it was because I was still a child myself; I could relate more to them. But I think it was my focus on the children. I had little else to distract me, and the adults had more that distracted them in their busy lives.

This program was a very new concept, and there wasn't much in the way of special equipment, at least not much the school or the parents could afford. The families came up with all kinds of ways to make their child's life better. I remember one family cut out a round plastic garbage can so that it could be used as a special chair for their child who had very little head and trunk control. He was basically like a rag doll. To support him, the front of the garbage can was cut open and a towel was placed in it for comfort. The round back gave the child enough support that he wouldn't fall over. They carried him around in it, and he could sit up in it to see the world better. Now, we have (outrageously expensive) seats that are similar to this that can be used. Much of the adaptive equipment we have today was designed by desperate parents looking for a way to make their lives and the life of their child better.

This was long before the laws were created to educate all children. This meant public school was not responsible for having classrooms available for children with disabilities. I remember a sweet little girl, very long and skinny, severely physically impaired but very responsive. She enjoyed coming to school so much! But she was getting older, and she was aging out of the preschool program we provided. On her last day she was allowed to attend, her mother cried uncontrollably. The child was now too old for the preschool, but there was no public school designed for a child like her. So she would now be relegated to staying at home every day, with no children or activities to keep her motivated and developing. Thank goodness that has changed, and schools are now required by law to have appropriate classrooms and educational programming for all children.

Over the summers, I became very comfortable in the classroom and fairly knowledgeable about teaching techniques with the children. I even got paid one summer $1 an hour and made close to $400 over the summer. I thought I was rich. Many times, I was put in charge of lesson plans and simple therapy with the kids. Today, it would be considered dangerous for a volunteer to do some of the stretching and therapy I was doing with the children. Now, only licensed professionals are allowed to do many of the things I was doing at fifteen and sixteen years of age. Luckily, nothing bad ever happened, and it gave me confidence when the things I tried with the children were successful. I really felt that even the small things I did for them made a difference in their development.

I was always critical of the teaching staff and believed they weren't devoting enough time to the children's development. There seemed to be way too much wasted time. I was young and very enthusiastic and felt like they should be doing more. I decided to apply for a job there and skip college, and I remember telling my mother that I didn't need college; I already knew how to run a classroom and what to do with the kids so I could be a full-time teacher assistant, right now! I knew I could do a better job than many of the teachers that were there.

My mom gave me the best advice ever by asking a question. She asked, "Would you want those teachers telling you how to run the classroom, or would you want to be in charge so the classrooms would be run to your satisfaction?" If I wanted to be in control of the care the children received, then, I needed a special-education teaching degree to back me up. I knew she was right, as most moms are, and I decided to enroll in college so that I could do what was best for these children that I loved so much. However, there was one problem; no money for college.

Baby Tina with Aunt Alice, Uncle Johnny and sisters

Uncle Johnny with his girls

The family with Tina at Gran's house

Me at age 10 with my mom

# Chapter 2

## *Eyes on the Prize*

*"I know the plans I have for you," declares the Lord,*
*"plans to prosper you and not to harm you, plans to*
*give you hope and a future."*

—Jeremiah 29:11

After graduating from Sandalwood High School with mediocre grades, I enrolled in the local junior college. I worked part-time as a waitress to cover my class fees. My parents simply couldn't pay for me and my brother to both attend. There were no scholarships or other funds that I qualified for, but my drive and stubbornness got me through. I know God got me through, as well.

This was the first time I'd been on my own and began to trust God for the first time, as well. I had to work to raise funds all through college and took out way too much in student loans. But my eyes stayed on the prize. I got my associate in arts degree at the local community college and, then, transferred to the University of Florida. I worked after classes every day at a childcare center in Gainesville.

I actually didn't think I would enjoy it because these were children without handicaps. They were all after school students that would come from public school. I fell in love with them, of course, and enjoyed my two years there so much. It, actually, was the perfect complement to my earlier training. God knew I needed this background, as well, for the work He was preparing me to do. In the future, the skills to work with children of all abilities—children with and without handicaps—would be extremely important and skills I would need every day. Looking back, it is really something to see how much the circumstances in my life were obviously led by God. He was laying the groundwork for the work He intended me to do.

I took summers off to work full-time at the childcare center, as well as jobs waitressing, so it took five years to get my four-year degree, but I got it. I finally received my special-education teaching degree and all privileges that come with it—none.

In May of 1985, I walked across the stage in my cap and gown to applause, ready to take on the world. Much to my dismay, the next week, I was back waiting tables and serving pizza. I applied for a teaching position with Duval County and waited for my dream job to come along.

I even enjoyed the waitressing, though, knowing that a future job was on the horizon. I would get paid to do what I loved. I was married by this time and worked at the local Pizza Hut with my husband in the back, making pizza, and my future sister-in-law, waiting tables with me. We were all young and full of anticipation for what the future would bring.

By that August, I had been offered a job at Mt. Herman Exceptional Student Center. I would be teaching children with the most severe and profound handicapping conditions in Jacksonville; ones with multiple handicaps—physical, mental, and medical, as well as vision and hearing deficits. I think when they hired me, they weren't sure if I wanted this position. These were children not every first-year teacher would be able to handle or would want to. Little did they know, this was right up my alley!

The job at Mt. Herman was the perfect job for me with children that had the most severe challenges. I had been with special kids like this my whole life, and of course, I had that teaching degree to back me up and, after passing the teaching exam, my teaching license too. I walked in to classroom number "12," full of anticipation and excitement. Then, I saw a pile of therapy equipment in the middle of the room that I had never seen before and a list of children's names that would be my students in less than a week, and I panicked. These children were real, and they each would have parents that would expect me to fix them and know how to teach them, and suddenly, all my education seemed like useless book knowledge. I felt I hadn't learned anything of practical value. In a few days, there would be eight little people coming through the classroom door that I had never met, and they would be my responsibility. I had never felt so completely inadequate in my life. But it would not be the last time. Trusting in God and in myself would become a very valuable tool.

Don't let anyone think less of you because you are young, be an example. (1 Timothy 4:12)

As I set up my classroom, with help from my very experienced teacher assistant, I gained confidence. She explained how the equipment could be used and how the teacher before me had set up the room. I was given notes on the children and information from each child's individual education plan (IEP), and before I knew it, my book knowledge began to kick in. My college classes had not been a waste of time after all! Luckily, I had a few years of hands-on experience as well.

I was asked to help that year on a new curriculum for children with profound disabilities and to come up with a breakdown of the steps to teach the children the sequential objectives toward goals in each developmental area. The areas of motor, cognitive, speech, self-help, and social were addressed to help the children reach their fullest potential in each of the most important areas of child development. These were goals that were practical for a child to function more independently as adults. Goals were well thought through so that time would not be wasted teaching something a child might not need later on in life.

Each teacher was given a set of goals and smaller objectives to work on, practice with our students, and tweak to make the curriculum the best it could be as a teaching tool. This was a direct application of my college education to real classroom activities. Each objective was to be turned into smaller steps that even the most severely delayed child could learn so the steps could be put together into an accomplished goal over time.

It might seem too overwhelming to teach a child to feed themselves a meal, but they could be taught to just hold the spoon and then gradually taught to lift it and then to put it into their mouth and so on. Every child could learn bigger goals if we started out with simple objectives broken into tiny steps and practice it over and over again.

My dream to make a difference in the lives of these children was becoming reality! I worked very hard to make my classroom the most successful room at Mt. Herman. Even though my students were severely delayed, I taught them the small steps that would lead toward accomplished goals and did so with tireless effort. I was energized by the potential success of my students and just the possibility of one of them accomplishing a goal that no one expected. It would be especially rewarding if they accomplished a milestone that doctors had told their parents they couldn't accomplish. The anticipation of seeing a miracle made all the hard work worthwhile.

> Whatever you do, work heartily, as for the Lord
> and not for men, knowing that from the Lord
> you will receive the inheritance as your reward.
> (Colossians 3:23–24)

These children and their little lives were my responsibility; their parents were depending on me to make things better, so of course, I didn't waste a minute of the day. My teacher assistants (later called paraprofessionals) would come back from lunch, expecting me to be relaxing after a busy morning, and I would be working with a child on standing, or toy play, or communication. If the children were awake, then, I was stimulating them in hopes to get those brain pathways working better.

I wasn't doing it to prove anything; I really just enjoyed it. I was young and full of energy embarking on a new career.

I remember my mom coming to visit the classroom one day. She enjoyed seeing all the work I was doing as a real teacher and meeting the eight children that were my students. She later told me that one of my assistants asked her why I was working so hard all the time. She said, "Amy acts like there is somebody watching her all the time." Actually, I knew someone was. I knew God was there, and if no one else was looking at how hard I was working, God was. He was the only one I needed to please. It made me feel good—and still does—to know what I am doing with my life is pleasing Him.

> Don't lay up treasures for yourselves, where moths and rust can consume and where thieves break in and steal. (Matthew 6:19)

My brother, Marc, once told me how he felt about children with special needs and the gifts they bring. Marc volunteered alongside of me when we were kids and, eventually, became a pediatric physical therapist himself. He said, "There are a lot of jobs we can do that give rewards, monetary and otherwise. Yet working with these precious children is not rewarding at all on the surface. The kids can't even tell you, 'thank you' for the things you do. Many of them can't even give a smile at the appropriate time for your efforts, and their accomplishments may be small, but that is the kind of work that only

God can reward, and His rewards outweigh and outlast any immediate reward from the world." Marc was so right!

He had realized this while he was doing therapy with an older student. To help her gain strength, he was dancing with her and having to support her quite a bit. She was a nonverbal child that didn't respond much with facial expressions either. She may not have even understood the activity and certainly didn't understand the effort it took Marc to hold her up. While they were dancing, he realized that this is the work that pleases God. It's the kind that you don't do for any reward at all. No reward, other than a warming of the heart, knowing it's the right thing to do.

> Therefore, my dear brothers and sisters, stand firm. Let nothing move you. Always give yourselves fully to the work of the Lord, because you know that your labor in the Lord is not in vain. (1 Corinthians 15:58)

> For it is God who works in you to will and to act in order to fulfill His good purpose... And then I will be able to boast on the day of Christ that I did not run or labor in vain. (Philippians 2:13, 16)

My second year, I was promoted to a bigger classroom with much "higher-functioning" children. These children had slightly higher IQs and were expected to gain more independence. They might even test out of Mt. Herman one day and go to a center for trainable or educable children. This was considered a better position to teach children that could learn more. My hard work had paid off. My new classroom space was much larger and had been remodeled with state-of-the-art equipment and fancy decorations. Each child had a nice laminate cubby for their items and a special slot under it for their wheelchair to be parked. It was swanky for a special-education classroom.

I also had an office three times as big as my old one, and a big bathroom for toilet-training the children connected to the room, with shiny blue tiles and porcelain bathtubs just in case the kids got messy. In my old classroom, there was no bathroom at all. I had emptied a storage closet and put training potties in it for a makeshift bathroom. When children used the potty chairs, I had to pull out the removable "pot" and run it down the hall to empty into the real toilets in the restroom a few rooms away. This was not ideal, but it worked, and children did get trained.

The children in the classroom were fun and full of personality, and I enjoyed my new status. It would be a short-lived two years in that class, however, as my new principal expected certain things from me after the first year. Those things included helping her with documentation on undesirable staff. The way this was being handled didn't sit well with me, and I just didn't want to go along with it.

Needless to say, my fourth year at Mt. Herman, I was back in room "12" with no warning, no explanation, and with children even more severely delayed than before.

Now, this may have just been coincidence and timing, but it was an obvious demotion with no reason given, and my performance had never been questioned or corrected.

> Likewise you younger people, submit yourselves to your elders. Yes, all of you be submissive to one another, and be clothed in humility, for God resists the proud, but gives grace to the humble. Therefore humble yourselves under the mighty hand of God, that He may exalt you in due time, casting all your care upon Him, for He cares for you. (1 Peter 5:5–6)

I had done some amazing things while in the new class. I did co-teaching with the teacher next door. We had organized field trips with the students, even an overnight trip to Sea World. We did a Thanksgiving play with the students in costumes on an actual stage in the gymnasium. I planted a vegetable garden outside of the classroom and had big successes with all of the students. I was truly devastated that I would be moved in what seemed like punishment, with no warning or any discussion about why. I walked into "my" office to find out it was not mine anymore from a staff member. It was a blow, for sure, to my ego. A lesson that would serve me well in the future. We are not always in control, and maybe, I needed a reminder of who was.

After the shock wore off, I took this lowered status as a challenge to work harder than I had before. My students were so severely mentally delayed that year, they didn't even meet the criteria to qualify for speech therapy. Things were changing with funding in the schools and not all children could qualify for therapy services.

You would think that if you were a child in school and you couldn't talk that some form of speech therapy would be automatically given. That sadly is not the case, and still is not, with any therapy. Children have to qualify and show that they can improve and must show continued progress to keep getting therapy services.

Just because the children couldn't talk wasn't enough to show they needed speech therapy. They had to show they were smart and that the level of speech was lower than their mental capability. Certain skills were needed to prove that they were capable of communication and their speech or language level didn't match their cognitive level. None of my twelve students could respond by imitating actions or making choices, none could point or had any type of a "yes/no" response. In other words, in the eyes of the state, they would never learn to communicate, and speech therapy would be a waste of time and educational dollars. So I started working on teaching these pre-communication skills to my students. By the end of the year, eleven of the twelve children in my classroom had qualified for speech therapy.

It was a huge victory and showed me that anyone can overcome a negative situation, when setting your heart on doing what is right in the eyes of God. The greatest part of this victory was that I was voted as Teacher of the Year, that year, by a vote from the teaching staff at Mt. Herman. Many of the teachers that voted for me were much older and more experienced. It was quite an honor to have been voted best teacher by the other teachers at the school. My principal escorted me to the Teacher of the Year dinner to help me accept my award. I hadn't fallen apart when adversity hit me. I wasn't used to failure, so it was not easy for me to walk through the halls, knowing I had been, very publicly, put in my place. It was truly a reward from God.

Something I saw as a punishment and demotion—moving from a classroom I loved to one thought not as desirable—became a blessing. It lit a fire under me and made me prove to myself and others it wouldn't slow me down. I was a teacher no matter where I was placed and would find a way to shine. The school had demoted me, but God promoted me. What could be better than that?

> No one from the east or the west or from the desert can exalt themselves. It is God who judges; He brings one down, He exalts another. (Psalm 75:6–7)

> Come now you who will say, "Today or tomorrow we will go to such and such a city, spend a year there, buy and sell and make a profit;" whereas you do not know what will happen tomorrow. For what is your life? It is even a vapor that appears for a little while and then vanishes away. Instead you ought to say, "If the Lord wills, we shall live and go and do this and that." (James 4:13–15)

# CHAPTER 3

# *God Is Calling*

*However, there is a God in heaven who reveals mysteries... This was your dream and the visions in your mind while on your bed.*

—Daniel 2:28

*Not that we are sufficient in ourselves to claim anything as coming from us, but our sufficiency is from God.*

—2 Corinthians 3:5

I was at the top of my game at Mt. Herman. Things were great and could have continued to be so for many years to come. I had ended the '88–'89 school year with a bang by winning teacher of the year for my school. After all of my hard work had started to pay off, it would have been smooth-sailing for many years to come. After four years of teaching, I had become eligible and applied for tenure. I was married to my high school sweetheart in 1983 and had given birth to our first son, Zachary Jacob, four years later. I had a great marriage,

36

a wonderful little boy, a terrific job; basically, I had the perfect life. Why would I want anything else? Why would I leave this job where I was successful? Why would I rock the boat of life?

During that year, however, God started working out His plan. I might have been in a comfortable position, but God doesn't always want us to stay comfortable. One of the extra projects at the school had drawn my attention. I had agreed to chair a committee of teachers to do some research on services in Jacksonville. Services that would help our families at Mt. Herman. We thought it would be a good idea to create a handbook for them of businesses that would accommodate the special needs of their children. Our families faced problems like no others. They had questions that most of us would never think about.

"Will the local dentist be able to clean my child's teeth without sedation, and will they understand the complications that my child's seizure medications might cause if sedation is necessary?"

"Does my pediatrician know how to care for my child with a rare diagnosis, and are they even willing to do so and be supportive?"

"Can I simply walk into the hair salon around the corner to get my child's hair cut when they are in a wheelchair and have poor head control due to cerebral palsy or complex communication challenges and difficult behaviors to manage due to autism?"

These were questions our families faced every day, and the handbook would make their day-to-day lives a little easier. It sounded like a very worthwhile endeavor and one I had time to do along with my regular teaching duties.

The group began making phone calls to local owners and managers to compile our list, and we came up with many willing and able businesses, but the one thing we discovered was that no day care owners agreed to be on our list at all. They were afraid of the risk, and though some might not have been fearful, they simply felt they didn't have the training to give the children with special needs a quality childcare experience. Some might take a child with a slight delay but not one with more severe disabilities like the children at Mt. Herman. The biggest problem is that most childcare programs won't take children that aren't potty-trained by age three. Most of our students stayed in diapers for much longer and some for their entire lives. Even when they had the understanding, they couldn't sit up well enough to go on a conventional toilet seat. This leaves even children with slight developmental delays unable to attend most centers.

I had also spoken with many of the mothers that had been unable to work or finish school since the birth of their son or daughter. No day care meant no way to hold down a job or finish school. And many admitted, with embarrassment, they were living on welfare and food stamps. It was a stark reality for our families. This was their child, and somehow, it had never been considered that they should be able to continue living the life they had planned. Many parents of children with special needs hold onto unwarranted guilt about their child's disabilities; did this mean society deemed them guilty as well? It was almost as if they were being punished by society because they had given birth to a child with a disability. No one would ever admit this, but why was the burden placed solely on the parents when, most times, they were overwhelmed by the sudden responsibility placed on them.

This, in turn, punished the child, as well as any other children in the family, by keeping them in a financial disaster. This situation also prevented the child from being in a program with other children. While isolated, children with developmental delays lose the chance to learn from other children their age and become more delayed socially, as well as academically. The other side of this problem is that other non-handicapped children don't get to learn about and from children that are differently abled. If young people aren't exposed to children with challenges, how can they ever learn to feel comfortable with them later on and understand the challenges and gifts that children with disabilities have? This is a problem that carries over into our future society and dictates how adults with disabilities will succeed or fail.

Some could find grandparents or other family members willing to babysit during the day, but many of the children were too much for elderly relatives to handle. Family was, at least, a safe alternative, if they were available. Others chose to leave their child with neighbors or anyone willing to babysit to earn a few extra dollars. This was a terrible alternative as the untrained sitters gave the child no stimulation or activity during the day.

One mom told me her child was always sitting, staring at the same corner every time she came to pick her up. Her daughter was nonverbal, and it was obvious that she sat all day with no activity or interactions with the sitter. This mother felt even more guilt about the situation but had to work and felt she had no other option. This was the worst thing for a child that was already developmentally delayed. Many of these sitters were unlicensed and, therefore, not inspected or background screened. This was not only an education issue but one of risking children's safety as well. Desperate parents were pushed into unsafe situations for their child.

> Rob not the poor because they are poor: neither oppress the afflicted in the gate: for the Lord will plead their cause and spoil the soul of those that spoiled them. (Proverbs 22:22–23)

> "For the oppression of the poor, for the sighing of the needy. Now I will arise," says the Lord; "I will set him in the safety for which he yearns." (Psalm 12:5)

This, of course, reeked of injustice to me! These parents were victims along with their children in a world that, perhaps, didn't see it as the parent's fault but certainly saw it as their responsibility—alone. How could we live in this great country and in the huge city of Jacksonville, Florida, without someone coming up with a solution to this problem?

Most people I have spoken with over the years are shocked that there aren't government-funded programs that take care of problems like this. They assume that there is funding available and, until it happens in their family, are oblivious to the lack of help there is for families in these situations.

Wouldn't it be better if there was a day care with trained staff able to give kids with delayed development the therapeutic activities they needed to help them improve? Wouldn't it be better for society if these kids reached their full potential and gained as much independence as possible? Wouldn't it be better for the whole community to have the parents of these children working full-time to support themselves and contributing to the system, not just take from it? I couldn't believe that this problem had not been addressed.

My brain had been kicked into gear, and I am sure God was doing most of the kicking. He continued to place this situation before me as parent after parent kept asking if I knew of a childcare that would take kids with disabilities. I remember one parent in particular that called me on the phone to ask my advice. I was called to the front desk at school, and there was a mom on the other line, hoping I had an answer for her situation. She was about to lose a potential job because she couldn't find a day care that would take her daughter. Her daughter was severely physically and mentally delayed and in a wheelchair. The company wanting to hire her needed her to work full-time into the afternoon, but her child would be home from school before the end of her shift. As a public school, Mt. Herman let out at 2:30 p.m., and then, children were sent home on school buses. Her daughter would arrive sometime around 3:00 p.m. to 3:30 p.m., and as with most jobs, she wouldn't get off until 5:00 p.m. That meant she wouldn't be home until 5:30 p.m. at the earliest. She was desperate, and she expected me to know the name of a center that could handle her child's special needs. After all, I was the head of the committee that was supposed to find services for our families. I felt completely useless as I admitted to her that there were no childcare centers that I knew of that would take a child with the severe disabilities like those her daughter had. God had started to whisper to me that I could do something about it. Maybe, there was a solution to this problem, but no one else had stepped up and created it.

I suddenly started feeling responsible for fixing this situation. Like this mom's situation, it seemed like there should be a few daycare centers in Jacksonville that would take kids, at least for a few hours after school. There should be a few centers that could hire an extra trained staff member and just charge more money for it. Why hadn't anybody done it? Why not? Why not me?

The thought sounded ridiculous to me, at first. How could I do something that crazy on my own, when no one else was doing it? It would have been so easy to tell myself it was enough to work in a public school, teaching children with disabilities. After all, so many people had been telling me I was wonderful for becoming a special-education teacher. That I must be a special person to be able to work with "those" type of children. Just working with disabled children was difficult enough, right? I was doing my part by working in a field that few chose and many backed away from because it was too hard. I could do just as much good helping these kids in the public school and be a Christian witness there.

Telling myself those things worked for a little while, but God wasn't giving up. He had designed me with a brain that didn't shut off that easily. Everyone that knows me will attest to it. It is how God made me, after all. Once I started thinking about the idea, it wouldn't go away. I am not sure if this trait in me is a quality or a flaw, but it's just how I am. I'm sure my family would vote for "flaw," hands down!

I began to play with the idea in my head and ran different scenarios through my mind every chance I got. I kept a legal pad beside me to jot down ideas as they came and started coming up with a plan. It became almost like a hobby or pastime. Just kind of a game for fun, at least, that is what I told myself.

> God spoke to Israel in visions of the night and said, "Jacob, Jacob." And he said, "Here I am Lord." (Genesis 46:2)

The scenarios always were like a pipe dream, completely out of the realm of possibility. I was not thinking seriously about it—just thinking. I have to admit that when I thought about it, the childcare was just a business and not a ministry. The idea of helping people was more of a way for me to be an entrepreneur and to be able to keep my almost-two-year-old son with me more. As I thought more about it, I considered opening up my home to families. I could have Zachary there and turn the front of our very small Murray Hill home into a childcare area. I actually called a liability insurance company to find out about coverage, and the agent basically laughed at me and explained the annual cost would be extreme. This made me think that my idea was ridiculous, and I should quit thinking about it altogether.

But there was a part of me that was secretly hoping I would eventually hit on a formula that made sense because I really wanted to do it.

I would no sooner quit thinking about it, and God would whisper again. I thought about it so much that I began talking about it at work. A teacher at school that had heard me talk about it had mentioned my idea about a special childcare center to some of her parents. One of them had a room full of therapy equipment that her child had outgrown and was no longer using. She approached me and wanted to donate it all to me in hopes that I might really have a program one day. I accepted the offer, and she brought the items to school the next day. I loaded down my car with a large therapy ball, a corner chair, a therapy wedge and roll. These items became part of the furniture in my house. My son played on them for a while. He even enjoyed eating breakfast seated in the corner chair with the tray. It was perfect for cartoon watching. Eventually, the fun of using them wore off, and he forgot about them. They sat and sat and sat and became dusty.

One night, I went to sleep with the unused equipment still in the corner of my living room; my idea had completely stalled. But I kept the equipment just in case! The next morning, I was awakened by a very real dream. I dreamed that I *had* started a childcare center for kids with disabilities. The school was full of equipment and children and was in multiple rooms. These were not rooms in my house but rooms in a church. The rooms in my dream were Sunday-school rooms. I am not sure how I knew because they were not rooms in my church, Lakewood United Methodist Church. They weren't rooms from any of the places where I had volunteered as a teen. I didn't recognize them at all; I just, somehow, knew they were Sunday-school rooms. I walked through the rooms and saw my school with several classrooms, just like I had been planning on paper.

As I woke fully, the dream stayed with me. I realized how much sense my dream had made. God wasn't just whispering now; He was getting a little louder. He was getting harder to ignore. I actually started believing it could be real. It seemed more possible after the dream. I had actually seen it—in my mind, anyway. But dreams are pretend and just imagination; just your brain playing while you're asleep.

> I will keep watch to see what the Lord says to me
> and how He will respond to my complaint. Then
> the Lord said to me, "Write a vision and make it
> plain upon a tablet." (Habakkuk 2:1–2)

This dream *was* different. Most dreams are strange and bizarre and don't usually line up with reality. But this one made sense. Now, my planning got a little more serious. I could actually visualize this dream coming true. My idea seemed a little more practical. It was still completely crazy but slightly less crazy. If I run my school in a church building, they would have insurance, other possible resources, and more room than in my house. I began to put pen to paper again and think about the logistics of my childcare.

I crunched numbers of what parents would pay for this service. It was, after all, a service that would be invaluable to a family that really needed it, and they would probably be desperate for childcare. I could keep Zachary with me during the day, and that would save money. I remember the original amount was around three hundred dollars a month for the service, full-time, and I calculated the number of children I could care for and the extra staff I would hire. I considered I would keep half the money for my salary, and the other half would go to some teacher assistants and operating expenses. It's funny now, I don't think I knew terms like operating expenses, and I guess this would be considered a business plan, but I'm sure I didn't know then what a business plan was at all. These terms are all very familiar now. After all, I had a special-education degree, not a business degree. I was never even planning to teach math to my students. It was completely out of my skill set. And "yes," I did come to use all the math I learned in high school.

I wrote a letter to share my idea with my church, Lakewood United Methodist. I guess that was my business proposal—another term I didn't understand at the time. I still didn't know, at all, what I was doing and looking back is really proof of my lack of business knowledge and how really unprepared I was to venture into something like starting a childcare. Because of my dream, I considered presenting the proposal letter to my church.

Lakewood United Methodist Church had been my church since I was born. My grandparents and parents were longtime members. My parents, my brother, and I were baptized and married there. I even went to kindergarten at Lakewood Methodist and spent many Sundays and weeks of vacation Bible school in the rooms of the Sunday-school building. My parents had even been Sunday-school superintendents for many years there. This would be the perfect place to start my day-care center, and those rooms had not been used during the week since they closed the kindergarten years ago. Once kindergarten had become part of the public-school system, there was no longer a need for churches to provide private kindergarten. It was now free for families, so most wouldn't pay for the church programs anymore. I was sure this was God's plan to put these rooms to use in the church I had always known. I would have the support of my church, and that made perfect sense to me. It would be a safe place to start; a familiar place with familiar people.

Even though I had thought all this through and had put my thoughts on paper, this idea had me terrified. I had a good-paying, secure job with fantastic benefits doing what I loved. I had holidays and summers off and got off work by 3:00 p.m. each day. My husband was not exactly raking in the money himself, so we depended on my paychecks very much. Of course, I had calculated my pay at half the income my day care brought in, but what if no income came in for a while—maybe, a long while.

We also would have no health insurance as my husband's job didn't offer it. What was I thinking? Well, maybe, I wasn't thinking, or maybe, God was still whispering thoughts in my ear, encouraging me. Whatever the reason, I met with the board of trustees at Lakewood and presented my idea. I was nervous but felt emboldened because I knew many of these people. They had helped raise me as elders in the church.

They were very receptive and pleasant. After all, they had all known me since I was a child. The presentation was going along very smoothly right up until the end. There was one little glitch. They had just signed a contract with someone else to use that space for a regular preschool program. I was too late! I was devastated that after all this time, I had just missed the opportunity that someone else was getting. She wasn't even a church member. Was this a case of really bad timing, or was God closing a window so He could open a door? This is not typed backward, by the way. I was very disappointed and figured that was the end of that, or was it?

My husband and I had moved to the Murray Hill neighborhood in 1987. We loved the old houses, and even more important, we could afford them. This made the cute little bungalows even more attractive. With both our paychecks, we were able to afford a small home with two bedrooms and one bath. We had saved up a small down payment for the mortgage while living with his mom for a year. I had hoped to own a home before having children, and we had just bought our first home right before our first child was born.

I really wanted to attend church with our newest addition and raise him in the church as I had been. So Lakewood United Methodist was the only church I knew. As time went on, it was a struggle to drive all the way to Lakewood to go to church.

Lakewood was about ten miles from our new neighborhood, and we got lazy about going regularly. The distance may have been just an excuse, but we also were struggling to find our place there. As a child, I fit in fine, but now, as an adult with a young family, there didn't seem to be a place for us.

My husband and I tried volunteering. As an actor with a degree in theatre, we were sure they could use my husband's talents, along with my teaching experience. This, however, was not the case, and we ended up in an area with youth, not children and not theatre. It was an area neither of us felt very comfortable. We were barely older than the youth we were given to mentor. We even felt that we weren't really needed in that position. We were stuck filling in between the planned activities to supervise basketball. This was not my or my husband's forte. We were actually miserable in the role we'd been given, and the kids just played ball and ignored us for the most part. All of these factors led to our lack of motivation about going at all.

At a garage sale one Saturday in our neighborhood, we ran into the mom of one of my Mt. Herman students. Matthew was a beautiful four-year-old blond headed boy, with Angelman syndrome. This is also called the "happy puppet syndrome" because the children flap their hands when walking, and they smile and laugh a lot. They are also quite mentally delayed, and many have seizure disorders, along with slow motor development. Their sweet smiles and pleasant disposition make them a joy to be around. Matthew was no exception. He was beautiful and sweet, and I loved having him in my classroom.

Matthew's mom was tickled to see me out in public and rushed over to talk about Matthew's progress in my class. She, then, asked if I lived in the neighborhood. When I told her we lived nearby, she immediately invited me to her church, Murray Hill United Methodist Church. I told her I had been raised Methodist, but I had grown up at Lakewood UMC and couldn't imagine myself anywhere else. She told us to think about it, anyway.

> We know that God causes everything to work together for the good to those who love God and are called according to His purpose. (Romans 8:28)

Well, we did think about it and realized if we attended a church closer to home, then maybe we would go more often. After all, Murray Hill UMC was only one and a half blocks from our house. This would leave no room for excuses that it took too long to drive there. We visited the next Sunday and fell in love with the people. Murray Hill was known as the "church of the warm heart," and it was true. We felt welcome and loved, but I was still struggling with leaving Lakewood. We actually didn't join right away, but Matthew's mom was persistent. She invited us a second time and said there was a new pastor at Murray Hill, and he was a great preacher. Her persistence paid off, and we obliged her by giving Murray Hill a second shot.

After the second visit, we decided we loved the people and the new pastor, Rev. Bill Fisackerly. Eventually, we moved our membership to Murray Hill and started attending there regularly in 1988. I thought this was a move purely out of convenience and was completely my idea. The whispers of God were getting louder and louder; I just didn't know it yet.

Several months after we joined Murray Hill, there was a class offered on the history of Methodism for new members and anyone wanting to learn more about Murray Hill church programs. My husband and I decided to go through the course that was led by Russ Peters, who was the activities director of the church.

At the end of the class, Mr. Peters told us about all the ministries and activities we could join within the church and added, "Or you might even want to start a new ministry."

I'm not sure if he was serious, but I immediately thought of my special childcare idea. As soon as he finished speaking, I timidly raised my hand. I told him that I did have an idea that I had been thinking about for a couple of years now. I was sure he would think I was crazy and my idea was too. It wasn't like there were other churches that had done such things. Many churches had childcare and preschool programs but not for children with handicaps. And besides, Murray Hill had a childcare program already that was up and running in two rooms of the Sunday-school building. This made it seemed even more unlikely that a new one, only for kids with handicaps, would be of any interest to the church.

To my surprise, he seemed genuinely interested, so I began to tell him about the kids at Mt. Herman and how the parents couldn't find childcare and how angry it made me that someone hadn't done something about this problem! I felt I could run such a center but needed some help getting it started. As I spoke, a strange look came over Russ's face. At first, I thought he was simply trying to find a way to say "no" to me gracefully. He began to tell me about his childhood. He had two brothers that were both handicapped and, when older, had been placed in institutions as was common at the time. One of the brothers had died in an institution. He had seen the struggles that his own mother had gone through. Russ had been in that family that had "always struggled financially." He could completely relate to the families at Mt. Herman I spoke about and on a personal level.

He looked me in the eye and said, "We are gonna do this, I want to help you to make this happen." Now, God was coming through loud and clear. This is why I had moved to the other side of town from where I had grown up. Why I had bought a house one block from a different United Methodist church. I had been invited to this church by a mom with a child with severe disabilities that I taught in public school. I had run into her in my new neighborhood. On top of all that, my husband and I took a class at this new church about programs in the church, which was presented by a man that had been in one of those struggling families I so wanted to help. He had first-hand knowledge of how difficult life can be for families with special kids. He would present the idea to the new pastor of the church, Reverend Fisackerly. My thought was not a positive one about what the pastor's reaction would be. I assumed he would put a stop to this idea before it went any further. It was an unusual ministry, to say the least, and one that came with obvious risks.

Now, there are some things that might be considered mere coincidence, but as the rest of this chapter of my story continues, even the most skeptical among us would reconsider believing in a higher power after hearing it. I lived this story, and I still have a hard time believing these events actually happened. It is my firm belief that there are no such things as coincidences, and certainly, this time, there was not one.

I had no idea how the pastor of the church would react. He was an older gentleman, and I assumed he wouldn't be interested in something new and something so unconventional. Most new pastors don't want to upset the apple cart, and I figured he would be happy with status quo. There was already a small preschool program on the premises, and would they even want another ministry in the building? And this was no ordinary ministry; it was something that hadn't been tried before; not in a Methodist church and certainly nowhere in Jacksonville. Would he be afraid of taking on children with handicaps, possibly even severe handicaps?

I was pretty sure that as head pastor, he would put on the brakes before we got the program rolling. As head pastor, he was probably more concerned with the problems that might arise that could hurt the church. The church members were probably his first priority, I assumed. And rightly so! This crazy idea would certainly sound even crazier to the head minister of the church.

The next day, I got my answer. Russ called me to tell me the news, and my heart was racing. During the night, I had completely convinced myself that the answer would be "thanks, but no thanks" for your sweet yet silly idea. When Russ told me the answer from the pastor, I was genuinely shocked! My concerns were completely unfounded. God was moving this along even faster and more obviously than I could have ever imagined. The pastor not only liked the idea, he was in love with it and wanted to help in any way he could. I couldn't believe my ears, but he was thrilled about the plan.

You see Reverend Bill had been raised around children with disabilities. His mother was a special-education teacher just like me.

She was one of the first special-education teachers trained and hired to work with children that were mentally and physically delayed back in the 1920s, right here in Jacksonville. Reverend Bill said that he would get out of elementary school before his mother was finished teaching at her special-education program for the day. The school allowed him to come in and sit quietly and do his homework. He would wait in the room while his mother completed lessons with her students. He recalls being amazed at her patience as she would go through the lessons with the children over and over until they understood. When he questioned why it took the children so long to learn lessons that seemed simple to him, his mother lovingly explained that the children's brains didn't work quite as fast as his did. She told him that if she kept repeating the lessons, then, the children could learn things just like him. It just took them a little longer, and we should never give up on them, just try again. He saw time and time again how the children did learn in spite of their conditions. His mother was not just a special-education teacher but one that was renowned for her teaching techniques and revolutionary methods she used for children with disabilities. He has brought me newspaper articles about his mother going to California to share her techniques with the teachers there.

Now, I understood his overwhelming reaction to my proposal. This was a ministry that was made for him and for this church. He was possibly even more excited than I was about the idea of a program for kids with disabilities in his church. I know he had his dear mother in mind and knew this would honor her if his church helped the children she loved so much. Now, I'm not sure if this was the exact church that I pictured in my dream, but it certainly was the one God had planned on. He had been planning this—now, I know—for decades. God was grooming little Billy Fisackerly to be open and ready for the challenge of starting a new program in his church one day. All those times he sat in his mom's class, watching her working with the special children, back over sixty years before, God was softening his heart toward kids with disabilities. Reverend Bill was learning that these children were able to improve, and they were valuable to our community through the gift God had given his mom to teach them.

All of the pieces were fitting into place, and this was the church! A church where a family that had been brought up at Murray Hill was now caring for a son with Angelman syndrome. And that child was a student of mine in public school. A church where the activities director of that church had two brothers that had been born with handicapping conditions, and now, a new head pastor with a special-education teacher for a mother. God had not only been preparing me, He had also been preparing this congregation to be willing to take on this ministry when I finally got around to starting it. God had just started shouting, "This is the place, Amy! Do you hear Me? This is it. Now, get moving on My plan, not yours, Mine!"

But was I ready to take that leap of faith and quit my job to do this? With the things that had lined up at Murray Hill, God made the choice pretty easy. It was obvious to me that He was part of this plan, and I had to put my doubts and fears aside. In a way, I had been "set up" by God or Murray Hill United Methodist church had been. The best thing to do when set up by God is go with it. But even though God set it up, that didn't mean everything from here on out would be easy. I had to get ready for the roller-coaster ride of challenges and blessings. I was very apprehensive about the next step of faith, for sure. I guess, I figured fighting the obvious situation that God had given me would be more foolish than quitting my secure job at Mt. Herman. I was scared *not to* take the plunge.

> To Him who is able to do immeasurably more than all we ask or imagine, according to His power that is at work within us, to Him be glory in the church and in Christ Jesus. (Ephesians 3:20–21)

Me and son Zachary at age 2

Zachary watching TV on top of the "Corner Chair" in our home

# CHAPTER 4

# *Stepping Out in Faith*

*Many are the plans in a man's heart (or women's),*
*but it is the Lord's purpose that will prevail.*

—Proverbs 19:21

I began preparing my leave-of-absence notice to the Duval County school board and got busy thinking about my new program. I took the summer of 1989 off from work to start making plans. I put out the word to some families at Mt. Herman that I was going to start my childcare in the fall. I came up with a flier and found some clip art of a child in a wheelchair and a teddy bear in a stroller that looked like a pediatric wheelchair and did my best to spread the word. I chose the name Developmental Day Care, based on the old school program at United Cerebral Palsy.

I hoped this would convey that the program was intended for those children with developmental delay. Later changed to Developmental Learning Center (DLC) to make sure people knew it was more than just day care! The children would be learning too.

I had no connections at that time with the community and really had no idea how to find families that might need these services, other than the ones at Mt. Herman. I sent a few fliers to local pediatricians and around the neighborhood. I began setting up the room that the church provided for me, which was also the church nursery and one other Sunday-school room if I had enough children to need it.

Finally, the dusty therapy equipment that had been stored for so long at my house could be dusted off and have a new home. Now, I knew this was the home the donated items had been meant for, not my living room. They looked perfect in the corner of the church nursery and changed the look of the room. Now, the room looked like a therapy room. It was ready for children with challenges! But was I ready for all that lay ahead?

The church nursery was perfect because I could use the cribs that were used on Sunday, along with the toys, furniture, and phone that were available in the room. I simply added a few therapy-type toys that I bought at the dollar store. I bought some cheap stackable, colored cups, a Barrel of Monkeys set, and old Ants in the Pants game from my childhood, and some new play dough and was set to open. I got a Rubbermaid bin with a lid and started filling it with the items to use for therapeutic activities. I had no start-up money to buy needed items for the classrooms, so I had to be creative. I even used some golf tees and a block of Styrofoam as a simple peg set. It wasn't ideal, but all my supplies worked. I don't think they were up to code, and I'm sure the items, today, would be considered a safety hazard, but they were cheap.

I knew nothing about grants or fundraising. Looking back, I wonder how things would have been different if I only had some idea how to write a grant and had funding to help me get started. I had done very little preparation for the start of my venture. After all I've learned, I am sure things would have gone much easier, but I'm not sure it would have been better for me.

God knew to start me out small and let the program grow along with me. They say God doesn't call those that are able, just those with a willing heart. I know this to be true, and I know it was God because there is really no other way that the program worked and was successful. Other programs and even big businesses have come and gone while DLC just plugged along. There really is no other explanation. With God behind it and so many others that wanted DLC to succeed, we survived many dark times over the next decades.

Russ Peters had done the leg work while I was finishing up my year in public school at Mt. Herman. He even acquired the zoning permit to add more children during the week at the church property. These children would add to the numbers coming to the Murray Hill Preschool, housed in the same building. Russ had done the hard work; the only hard thing for me was to commit to turning in my letter of resignation to Duval County schools. That was the easy part yet hardest thing I'd ever done.

> Jesus looked at them and said, "With man this is impossible, but with God all things are possible. (Matthew 19:26)

Well, I did turn in my resignation to Duval County Public Schools during that summer, with some fail safes built in. I took an extended leave so I could go back if things didn't work out. I was not completely convinced that "all things are possible with God." Not yet, anyway. I believed it in my heart, just not my head. I have always thought it crazy that the Israelites still doubted God after they had seen the plagues of Egypt come to pass. Not to mention the parting of the Red Sea.

Our heads always get in the way of giving complete control over to God. After all the things that had happened leading me to this church, how could I doubt? Now, I understood the Israelites a little bit better. I did believe in the impossible enough to make it the DLC tagline. On all our fliers and brochures since the beginning, I have used the phrase, "DLC, 'where anything is possible.'" It's amazing that something I picked on day one seemed to be the perfect phrase for the ministry. I knew if this school was going to happen, it was because of God making it happen, and I also knew this would be an inspiration to the families of the children we would serve. Many of them have little hope of success for their children and, maybe, reading that statement on our brochures would remind them to give God a chance to change the impossible situation they were facing to a possible positive future for them and their child. It was clear God's plan for this program to be in a church made a lot of sense. Our families need the church, and the church needs a ministry where they can serve. It was a match made in heaven.

> What does it profit, my brethren, if someone says he has faith but does not have works? Can faith save him? If a brother or sister is naked and destitute of daily food, and one of you says to them, "Depart in peace, be warmed and filled," but you do not give them the things for which are needed for the body, what does it profit? Thus faith by itself, if it does not have works, is dead. (James 2:14–17)

Fliers continued to circulate around Mt. Herman and around town as best as I knew how to circulate them. By August, we were getting a small response. A young girl from Mt. Herman with severe disabilities and hearing loss had a mother that worked and was single. While pregnant, the mother had contracted a common virus—cytomegalovirus (CMV)—that causes birth defects. The earlier in the pregnancy that the virus is contracted, the more severe the birth defects can be. One of the main issues it causes is microcephaly or a small brain and head size. It's just like the Zika virus that is more well known today and spreads from person-to-person like a cold virus. CMV is very common, and symptoms are mild flu-like symptoms. Most people never know they have had it.

The mother had been leaving her daughter, Rhonda, with a neighbor and was unhappy with the environment. As is the case with many of the children, the lady taking care of her had no idea what to do with a child with disabilities, so she did nothing. Her mother would find Rhonda sitting in the middle of the floor of the house when she arrived to pick her up each day, with nothing to do. Mom felt guilty that she was so neglected all afternoon after school and wanted her to be with someone that would help her development and give her some fun experiences as well. Also, like many parents, she was told by doctors that Rhonda would never learn. She didn't believe her daughter could learn to care for herself, so she did everything for her. She never allowed Rhonda to do things for herself. Now, Rhonda was older, and her mom began realizing she could learn and didn't want to waste any more time.

The second family that contacted me had a one-year-old with tuberous sclerosis. This is a hereditary condition that a family can carry for generations in a mild form, and then, suddenly, it appears in a devastating form. This disease is similar to the elephant man disease, progeria, but the tumors grow on the inside. They also grow on the internal organs and in the brain, causing brain damage, seizures, and developmental delay. Her mom came by to visit the school and was very unsure if she could trust anyone to care for Camilla other than herself, but the family was in need of a second income, and she was ready to go back to work.

This was the story I heard multiple times. Most parents were terrified to leave their precious child with a stranger, even a trained stranger. Most of the families had not been sure their child would even live after they were born. They would watch the child every second to make sure they were okay at home. They didn't feel anyone could take care of this special baby like they did. As it would happen hundreds of times, this mom would leave her child for a couple of times a week for a few hours, at first, to see how it would go. I was being tested. I didn't mind because I knew I would pass the test. After a few days, parents who are, at first, terrified to leave their child behind soon realize that not only is the child going to be all right, they were actually doing very well. They were doing great, in fact. After a couple of weeks, they realize that the child they were afraid couldn't make it at day care was just fine. Then, they discover that this child is not only fine, they are thriving—even improving. Children that slept all day at home were awake and enjoying the activities and stimulation. Children that wouldn't eat were learning to get over their defensiveness to food. Children that weren't responding were beginning to smile and make eye contact. It was always the same, and it was that way right from the beginning.

Just having regular stimulation, a new environment, being introduced new food repeatedly, and having someone that expects them to improve can have miraculous results. These are things that simply don't happen at home very often. Parents have other responsibilities and don't have the training to know what to do. They often feel guilty about pushing kids too hard, and home is too quiet, accommodating, and familiar to be as stimulating as a school setting. Once a parent got more comfortable with the idea, a few hours a day a few days a week quickly would turn into all day five days a week. Parents are so relieved, at first, to have some help and to feel comfortable away from a child they have cared exclusively for since birth. It is wonderful to be able to give that break to a very stressed-out parent.

A parent with less stress is a much better parent. They also realized this was time well spent and knew their child really was learning and enjoying the time away. The children enjoyed it even more than the parents.

> Bear one another's burdens and so fulfill the law
> of Christ. (Galatians 6:2)

> Therefore comfort each other and edify one
> another. (1 Thessalonians 5:11a)

The other regular occurrence at DLC was the parent's pleasant surprise to our positive reaction to the children. Many of our parents had a fear of rejection for their child. So many people that are introduced to children with disabilities and children that don't look healthy are naturally hesitant when they first see them. When most people see any other little baby or small child, the response is usually one of smiles and joy for new parents. The common comment is "congratulations," followed by compliments about how cute and adorable the child looks. Parents of children with disabilities don't often get that response.

This can be a painful reminder to parents that there is something wrong with their child, something not normal. Parents were always surprised when I would show genuine pleasure at the sight of this child, which, to me, really did bring excitement and joy. I didn't have to fake it. My reaction was genuine. Not only am I used to seeing most types of disabilities, but to me all children truly are adorable, and my immediate inclination is to want touch them and hold them. I almost always would ask to hold the children right away, and I was told later by many moms that that made them feel so good from the start. In many instances, I think it made them feel better about their own child and not just about me and the program. To see my joy gave them joy and told them, maybe, this child was going to be all right.

The third child that was there from the beginning was my own. My two-year-old Zachary was our first inclusion child or "typically" developing child. Inclusion programming, or having children with and without special needs together, was unheard of at this time. Later, DLC would become the first full-inclusion preschool in Jacksonville. The law would encourage this down the road, but this was not the reason Zachary was there. Since I would have little or no income at first, I would pull my son out of childcare and keep him with me. It was really part of my original plan since I hated being away from him so much.

It was great to have him with me all day, but it was a challenge as well. He didn't understand sharing his mommy with these other kids and certainly didn't like me on the phone when I got a call. It was hard to do business with him there, but we both learned how to make it work. It was worth it to have him with me more while he was little, even if he didn't have my full attention. It all worked out, and he was able to go to Murray Hill Preschool when he turned three for a (three-hour) partial day. Murray Hill Preschool was the other children's ministry at the church. We shared the same building with them called Worley Hall. They were in two rooms on one side of the first floor, and we were in two rooms on the other side with a courtyard separating us.

The preschool was for three- and four-year-olds and had been there since the '50s. It had started out as a kindergarten and had changed to a preschool when kindergarten became part of the public-school system. Strangely enough, years later, I was shown an old class photo from one of my employees who had attended Murray Hill Kindergarten. As we looked at the children, we discovered one of her classmates had Down syndrome and, then, found out another child enrolled had a hearing aid and hearing loss. It seems like God had always had this plan for Murray Hill United Methodist Church.

Once the program got started, I realized how daunting a task I had really chosen. I had to get my son ready and be there in the morning by 7:30 a.m. and was there all day by myself, no breaks, no days off, no sick days, and I had to stay until the last child was picked up by 5:30 p.m. Of course, the parents always wanted to talk and discuss their child's day, and I wanted to tell them about progress made to encourage them. Then, I usually had more to do to clean up the classrooms and get Zachary ready to go. So I was never home before 6:30 p.m. That made for very long days, five days a week.

One time, I remember getting a stomach virus, and it was a doozy. I had vomited all night. By the time I had to be at the school, I had quit vomiting but was very dizzy and weak as I headed to work. There was no administration office to call into for a replacement teacher like I had done when in public school. There were no other employees that I could phone to work for me. There was no way to find a substitute teacher on short notice or long notice for that matter. I was the sole employee. There were no sick days, no vacation days, and no personal days. It was me, myself, and I as the entire staff from open to close.

Basically, all I did that day was watch the kids and kept them safe. I fed and changed them when I needed to but didn't do much in the way of play or therapy. I really don't know how I made it but got through it, somehow. When they went down for a nap, I remember lying on the floor, staring at the ceiling, and hoped it was an extra-long nap time that day.

I could have told the parents to keep the children home that day but just hated to do that. Then, they would be in a jam. I didn't want them to miss work as some had just gotten jobs. The parents never knew I was sick. I kept a smile on my face, and the children were happy and clean when they arrived to pick them up. It is amazing what we can endure when we the need arises.

After a couple of months, the word began to get around about the program and the special care the children were receiving. More children started enrolling, and I was able to hire a part-time assistant for the afternoon. I still stayed the entire day, from open till close, but now, I had help. It was nice just having another adult in the room to talk with and to share my ideas. We were up to six children; four all day and two after school.

It seemed like most of these children came with medical problems along with the developmental disabilities. This was not part of my plan. I found out that the other preschool programs in the area offered by Easter Seals and Cerebral Palsy of Jacksonville wouldn't accept children with a medical diagnosis.

I had never considered what I would do if children came with medical needs. At Mt. Herman, many of the children required medical care, and a nurse came occasionally to the rooms to take care of simple medical procedures. I had seen some of the care that was given. There were children that had medications given for seizures, others had tube feedings through the stomach, and some had breathing tubes in their trachea that needed suctioning. These were all very common medical situations that often accompany children with multiple handicapping conditions and genetic disorders.

I had never done a G-tube feeding but figured I could learn if the need arose. I also had seen tracheotomy care but knew I couldn't ever do anything like that. I had thought about it when the nurse did the suctioning treatment and told myself that was one thing I didn't think I could handle. I was glad there was a nurse there to take care of that job. As fate would have it, the next three children that came to enroll at DLC were either fed by G-tube or had a trach.

One of those three was a little guy that made it imperative for me to learn how to do tracheotomy care. This was a child that was abandoned at the hospital by a mother that wasn't capable of caring for his massive medical needs. He had been placed on a ventilator through a stoma (or hole in his neck) to keep him alive. He was now two years old and medically stable but still needed the trach and was also on oxygen twenty-four hours a day. There was a machine that pulled oxygen out of the air and condensed it so he would have the right amount to breath. He also came with another machine called a humidifier that was hooked up to him when he slept.

The really sad part was that he had never been out of the hospital because there were no foster families able to deal with the medical care he needed. One lady stepped up—a nurse from the hospital that had fallen in love with his perky, bubbly personality and wanted to take him home. However, she worked, and they needed childcare during the day if he was to ever get out of that hospital.

How could I refuse? She trained me to take on all the medical care he needed, which included suctioning his airway when it got blocked with drainage. As awful as that sounds and had always seemed to me, once I did it, it was no big deal. She told me, "It is just like wiping his nose," and it was really no different. I had to be brave enough to do it so he could breathe, and when a child needs to breathe, you find the strength to do what it takes to help. Really, when a helpless child needs something, one can find the strength to do anything.

Soon, the gastronomy tube feedings and suctioning of stomas became routine to me. They only slowed down the playtime and therapy temporarily. Then, we would get right back to teaching. The point is I was doing whatever was needed to get these children on the best path for development. My day was mostly filled with singing nursery songs, reading children's stories, toy play, and doing exercises with the kids that were physically delayed.

The biggest part of the day was lunchtime. Many kids with developmental delays and especially children that have a tracheotomy are very orally defensive. In other words, they are afraid to eat. Children born with developmental delay, especially those placed on ventilators at birth, are very sensitive in their mouth and throat, making swallowing difficult. Many times, a ten-minute meal can take an hour or more. With me there by myself, it was a slow process. Doing special exercises in and around the mouth to desensitize the area, before eating, helped the children accept the foods, but that took even more time. I tried every trick in the book and, sometimes, those that weren't in any book.

Older children that are learning to eat for the first time are often on pureed baby food, even if they aren't babies any more. But making it taste better would help. So I would add butter and salt to the baby food jar to make it more desirable. It may sound weird, but it worked. It was long and tiring but worth it to get them to eat more. We always got through it, somehow, and before you knew it, the children were eating much better and, oftentimes, even started feeding themselves.

Still, the days were long and lonely. I would be so thrilled to have adult visitors. Mostly, it was ladies from the church that would stop by to encourage me or just to play with the children. My favorite visitor, by far, was Joe. He was the gentleman that was the custodian for the church. He was there every morning, mopping, when I got there and always had something positive to say. He would check on me during the day to make sure I was doing all right and even would find items around town to donate to the school. Anything he saw that might be of use to me, he would haul over in his truck. He, many times, would check near the dumpster at St. Vincent's Hospital that was nearby. He found so many medical and office items that still had life left in them. I remember a huge floor-to-ceiling file cabinet, an examination table, and even an IV pole for us to hang the feeding bags from for G-tube feedings. He practically furnished the school for the first few years until we could afford to buy new items. Many of those items are still in use at DLC. Joe is no longer with us but still with me in spirit, and I think of him often. There would be no DLC if so many—too many to name—had not helped us at just the right time.

God was definitely with me, but that doesn't mean there weren't major struggles. My plan was to charge a fee for childcare and take half for my salary and the other half to pay for part-time staff and supplies. That was a great plan if we were fully enrolled, but with a handful of students, it wasn't enough to pay me much of anything. There seemed to be one major flaw in my original plan; most families had not worked since the birth of their child and were financially broke. Even if one parent had been able to work, most of the income had gone to medical expenses. I knew there was a need for a program like DLC, I just hadn't thought about the reality of these families and their financial situation.

By December, things were really bad. Money was just not coming in, and my loss of income had really hurt my family. We knew that Christmas was coming, and there were not going to be many gifts under the tree, if there was even going to be a tree. Someone had actually donated a box of food to me for Thanksgiving! I never thought I would be someone needing food donations. It was embarrassing, but I took it gladly and reminded myself this was all temporary.

This was a time of learning for me. There were, as you might say, many teachable moments. I was living through a difficult time, temporarily, what many people face on a regular basis. I became much more empathetic toward others than I had ever been. I didn't have to wonder how they felt; I knew firsthand now.

I had originally thought if things got extremely bad, I could sell my car. The church that housed the school was only a block and a half away from my house, and I could walk to work, if necessary. We really didn't need to have a Christmas tree either. I knew we had family that we could turn to if things got really bad. Many of the families we would be helping had no one to turn to when things got tough.

As the holidays approached, I began to panic and tried to figure out how to fix this financial disaster. I started to question myself about my choice of leaving teaching in public school. Maybe, I had been crazy, and this was all my idea. Maybe, I hadn't been called to do any of this. I really can't remember how long I had been in worry mode, when I finally realized I wasn't all alone in this. It hit me that I was trying to come up with a solution without including God. I immediately felt ashamed and began to pray for God's guidance. After the prayer, I started to relax about the money problems. A peace came over me, and I knew whatever happened, things would be all right. Now, this peace was not normal for me when it came to money problems. Before DLC, I would get into a frenzy just paying my personal bills. My husband even took over bill-paying so I wouldn't have to see the bills we couldn't pay. I was a chronic worrier.

This peace settled into my heart, and it seemed like only minutes had passed before the phone rang. It was the March of Dimes program director calling me. I had sent some information about the developmental day care I was starting, asking for their help. I had reached out to several agencies in the hope that some of them might want to make a donation to help out the school. If others liked the idea and saw a need, it might bring in funding to keep us going until more children enrolled. The lady on the phone explained that, normally, the March of Dimes only gives to groups who do preventative work and prenatal care to improve the health of unborn babies. She went on to say that after reading my information, she and her board felt my program was so needed in this community that they were going to bend the rules, and the board members had voted to give me five thousand dollars to help me get started. I almost jumped through the phone to kiss her. I couldn't believe someone was willing to give me that much money. It was approved for me to spend half the money on my salary, and the other half was to be spent on supplies for the school.

Now, I could pay my bills and buy some Christmas presents too. A church group from a local Methodist church donated a tree for me to take home to my little boy from their tree lot. It was scraggly, but it was free, and it was full of love from that church group, and that made it so beautiful to me.

Something else very strange happened that Christmas, and I still have no plausible explanation today as to what really happened. The "big thing" out that year was an Atari game system. One day, a box was delivered to the doorstep of my home and left there. It had our address on it but someone else's name as the recipient—a name we had never heard before. We called and reported that it had been delivered incorrectly and needed to be picked up by the post office. The post office said there was nothing they could do if it had our address on it and told us to keep it.

We didn't feel right keeping it, so we decided to look up the name on the package and take it to the rightful owners ourselves. Problem was the name didn't exist in the Jacksonville phone book. We had tried to do the right thing but had no idea what else we could do to get it to the family that ordered it. We decided to keep it and enjoy it and considered it a Christmas present from God. When God gives a present, He goes all out; this was the full system, with a robot you could control and everything. All the bells and whistles. It was one of the many times God helped in a big way at just the right time. Our Christmas that I had been feeling so gloomy about was suddenly looking wonderful. We had a very Merry Christmas for us and our little boy after all. God was beginning to teach me to trust in little and big things.

This was not the first time I got stressed out, trying to fix a terrible problem of which I couldn't see an answer. Then, after wrestling with all the solutions on my own, I would remember that I was trying to do everything in my own power again. I would think of God, say a prayer, and the phone would ring with a donation, or someone would walk through the door with an item we needed. It became the pattern that I counted on. Soon, the worrywart that I had been was no more. The biggest financial hole could stare me in the face, and I would expect God to intervene. I would calmly wait on Him and go about my daily activities with a smile on my face. If I couldn't figure it out, it must be a God problem! I was a difficult student to teach. My way was to handle problems on my own and find the answer based on my knowledge. But God often has other things in mind that we know nothing about.

> Trust in the Lord with all your heart and lean not on your own understanding; in all ways acknowledge Him and He will make straight your path. (Proverbs 3:5–6)

It almost was as if when I tried to reason something out and think of a person I could call for help or a plan that I could come up with to solve a problem we were having at the school, God wouldn't allow it to work. I think He wanted to train me to not be independent as I had been my whole life. I might think of a good plan, but He could come up with one that was great, not just for me but for everybody involved. He can see the big picture, and we can only see in the moment.

> And Peter answered Him and said, "Lord if it is You, command me to come to You on the water."
>
> And He said, "Come."
>
> And when Peter had come down out of the boat, he walked on the water to go to Jesus. But when he saw that the wind was boisterous, he was afraid; and beginning to sink he cried out saying, "Lord, save me!"
>
> And immediately Jesus stretched out His hand and caught him, and said to him, "O you

of little faith, why did you doubt?" (Matthew 14:28–31)

I realized the problem of funding would never go away with so many families that needed our program that were financially not capable of paying. How could they pay if they had not been able to work, and how could they work if they couldn't put their child in day care during the day. Someone suggested I should write a grant to the Methodist organization, "JUMMBO." I had no idea what they were talking about. I didn't really know what a grant was. I had heard of one, of course, but didn't actually know what one looked like. I certainly had no idea how to write one. On top of that, I didn't know what a JUMMBO was.

Today, finding this information might have been a little easier. But this was "BI"—before the internet—so I couldn't just go onto the internet and do a search on Google for a sample grant. I couldn't just research it and get a grant template. I had no way to look up what JUMMBO was all about or how they expected a grant application to look. I made a few phone calls to the people recommended by my pastor. They gave me an address to write to and told me to simply explain what DLC was trying to do in writing and tell them about our needs. I was told JUMMBO stood for Jacksonville United Methodist Mission Board, and this was a group that helped missions get off the ground. This is the moment I realized that my developmental day care was a mission, and if we could write grants to help the families afford the tuition, we were truly a charitable ministry.

I asked for enough money so that children could come for free, at least, in the beginning. This would allow children whose families couldn't afford the day-care tuition to be able to attend while their parents worked. They would then get back on their feet, financially, by holding down a steady job. Much to my surprise, the JUMMBO organization liked the idea of providing scholarships for children to attend for free. They sent us the very first scholarship money, and three students could come for a whole year at no cost to their families. We also had a local business sponsor another child for a year—and just like that, we were up to eight children attending. My program had changed gears but was right in line with what God had intended all along. DLC was now a ministry in every way.

Now, with more children enrolled, I needed more help during the day. I also had several more children with medical needs. The two new children, a boy and a girl, were both G-tube fed and had seizures. Another little guy was very bright but had a genetic disorder that caused his muscles to be tiny and weak, even in his face. He required a G-tube, as well, for liquids as swallowing them was not safe. He could choke when thin liquids went down the wrong way and into his lungs. All of them needed one-on-one assistance to learn to eat by mouth.

I was barely making a steady paycheck, and it was small. I was just starting to help pay for some groceries and a couple of bills at home. How could I afford to hire someone with any medical training? I put an article in the Methodist newsletter, asking for a volunteer with nurse's training. I got a response right away from a registered nurse that had temporarily stopped working to raise her children, and she said she could help out a few hours a day. It was just what we needed. Jan was a jewel and became a great friend. She was not only able to take care of the medical needs of the children, but it also seemed she was a born special-education teacher as well. She was great with the children, no matter how delayed they were, and really enjoyed the experience. As time went on, we needed her more full-time but couldn't ask her to work full-time for free. With her big heart, she agreed to work her regular volunteer hours, and I could pay her what I could for the extra hours I needed her. Jan was just one of the generous souls that helped to make DLC a success. Another godsent connection sent at the right time.

> "Who is greater, the one who is at the table or the
> one who serves? Is it not the one at the table? But
> I am among you as one that serves." (Luke 22:27)

Jan worked for us like that for several years. Sadly, she had to move when her husband was transferred for work. I lost touch with Jan after she moved up north. We communicated at first, and she had found a job, working in another program at a public school with severely disabled children. She was hooked on this work as well. The children and the work are infectious. Now, there had been another person recruited into this wonderful world of special education.

# CHAPTER 5

## *Faith Grows*

*I tell the things that I have seen and learned at My Father's side, and your actions also reflect what you have heard and learned from your Father.*

—John 8:38

*Then Jesus told them, "I tell you the truth, if you have faith and don't doubt, you can do things like this and much more. You can even say to this mountain, 'May you be lifted up and thrown into the sea,' and it will happen."*

—Matthew 21:21

Well, we had made it through the first six months, and to be honest, I'm not sure how. We were beginning to get better known and with a good reputation. Most of the families just stumbled onto us, somehow. I knew we were doing the right thing, I just was so unsure of how to go about it. I just knew that God wanted this program in this church to welcome children that most would not. The overjoyed reactions from parents made it very clear we were filling a need and relieving their stress while touching their spirits. Many had been hoping and praying for something like this to be available, but many more had completely given up on praying altogether. I wanted that to change by the fact that our program was in a church and started by the church. My hope was that it might give them faith in God again. For some, it might be their first encounter with a church and people of the church, and this experience would show that God is with them in a practical way.

> At that time the disciples came to Jesus and asked, "Who, then, is the greatest in the kingdom of heaven?"
>
> He called a little child to Him, and placed the child among them. And He said, "Truly I tell you, unless you change and become like little children you will never enter the kingdom of heaven. Therefore, whoever takes the lowly position of this child is the greatest in the kingdom of heaven. And whoever welcomes one such child in My name welcomes Me." (Matthew 18:1–5)

I knew I had taken on a much bigger task than I had first realized. I, of course, wanted to be a good special-education teacher and help with the children's developmental needs. But now, I was beginning to see how God expected me to represent the church and Christians as well. This was a way to reach parents and whole families for Christ, to help them to grow in their trust and hope in God along the journey on which they'd been placed. The path of parenting a child with a disability is a daunting one, and one that can't be done without faith. It became apparent that my job was to show them the love God has for them and make it real to them so they will turn to God during their difficult times ahead. Family after family came to enroll their child, and I had to help them keep their faith.

One of the first students we enrolled after the first of the year was Kimberly. Kimberly was a true miracle just by being there. She was born with what is called "anencephaly" or, basically, with no true brain. She had a brain stem but not much more. Kimberly's parents, Laura and Paul, may have been the true miracle. They were told by doctors at three months into Laura's pregnancy that she should have an abortion, but Laura couldn't do it. She felt like it should be up to God to end her baby's life. The doctors then told her the baby wouldn't live for more than a few hours after birth, but she didn't listen to that either. The doctors assumed the parents would just spend time with their baby and wait for her to die naturally, but they were not willing to give her up that easily. Laura told the doctors to do whatever it took to save Kimberly's life.

The doctors had no choice but to try and save the newborn. They did surgery to remove dead brain tissue that had grown outside the skull and sewed up the opening in Kimberly's head. Much to the surprise of her doctors, she did not die, and a few weeks later, her mother took her home. Kimberly was proving to be a fighter just like her mom. She had heard about our program and wanted her daughter to go to school. Laura said she visited DLC not knowing how we would react to her baby. To me, she was a cute little blonde girl with a slightly smaller-than-average head. I grabbed her and started doing therapy to see how well she could sit up. Laura said when I did that, she knew this was the right place for her little girl.

Kimberly fit right in with our other students, and Laura became a fixture as well.

She took it upon herself to figure out how we could bill for insurance and Medicaid so we could do more therapy with the children. She singlehandedly got us enrolled in Medicaid, and we began offering physical therapy at the center. One of the therapist from Mt. Herman did therapy for us in the afternoon when she got off from work. This was the first therapy service we offered, and this gave families the freedom from having to take their child to another appointment. Therapy was done at school while parents worked. It was also better for the children as they got to have therapy during their regular school activities, so it meant more to them, and they learned faster.

During her time at our school, Kimberly became a local celebrity due to a very sad national trial. A family wanted to harvest organs from their child with anencephaly before she died so the organs would be more useful to another child. If the child was allowed to die naturally, the organs might deteriorate and not be able to be transplanted in another child that needed them. Laura was called to testify and bring Kimberly to the courtroom to prove children like this could live. We still have the hard copy of the front-page news article from our local paper about Kimberly's trip to Tallahassee to show how alive she really was.

Kimberly not only lived, she began to progress in her development. She responded to commands, learned to sit up and make sounds. She also began to eat soft foods from a spoon and drink from a cup. When she heard her daddy's voice from across the room, she would light up with the biggest smile. When he picked her up, she would turn to him and put her mouth on his cheek for a kiss. Her play became more responsive, and we really hoped she would keep improving.

When Kimberly turned four, we had a big birthday party for her at DLC. We had cake, ice cream, balloons, and of course, the silly hats. Her mom forgot one thing—a camera. She said not to worry about it, but I ran home to get my camera and made the party wait. We took tons of great pictures with Kimberly and all her school friends. That was one of the best decisions I ever made. Sadly, Kimberly passed away in her sleep, ten days later, from a high fever that spiked in the middle of the night. The part of the brain that regulates temperature was missing in Kimberly, and her body would often get too hot or too cold. The fever was more than her little body could handle. She lived four years and nine days longer than the doctors predicted.

> Brothers and sisters, we do not want you to be
> uninformed about those who sleep in death, so
> that you do not grieve like the rest of mankind,
> who have no hope. (1 Thessalonians 4:13)

Kimberly was the first of many children we said goodbye to at DLC. It was sad for us each time. The grief is part of the job, but that doesn't make it easier. I have seen too many funerals with tiny caskets. The other side of the story is that we got to know a beautiful little soul in each one of those precious children. We got to share that sweet soul along with their families. Sometimes, we are the only other people that truly know these children like their families knew them. That is an honor and a privilege that few people experience. This allows us to be some of the only people that can really help the families with their grief. They know they are not alone in their sadness; we will miss their children too and can truly mourn with them. We also were able to give those children a real childhood and the fun of being kids, not just patients. Kimberly got to be a kid and do real kid things just like other children. She got to be with her peers and share experiences with others. She got to finger paint, play with dolls, wiggle to music at circle time, and best of all, have parties on her birthday! We also are giving the families great memories to keep forever.

That's real church. The people of God reaching out in real love to hurting people and making life better. Better for the children and families and better for us also.

I am telling you these stories straight from my memories of these angels that walked among us. I truly feel blessed that I get to keep those memories forever too.

A new commandment I give to you, that you love one another; as I have loved you, that you also love one another. By this all will know that you are My disciples, if you have love for one another. (John 13:34–35)

I in them and you in Me—so that they may be brought to complete unity. Then the world will know that you sent Me and have loved them even as you have loved Me. (John 17:23)

As the program grew, so did the opportunities for funding. The government program to assist families with special children was called The Developmental Disabilities Program. Their director heard about DLC and the learning program we had available to children with developmental delays. About a year after we opened, she called our school and asked if she could come to see our facility and find out more details. She saw the students and the quality attention they were receiving and liked what she saw. She realized this kind of program was so needed in Jacksonville and wanted to help. The director's name was Susan Jaskovich, and she helped us apply for funding through their program. She personally saw to it that we were approved for this funding. Once DLC was approved, we were able to bill a daily amount of "developmental day training" for each child.

The children that were enrolled in our childcare and receiving the play activities and therapeutic programming were now provided with regular funding. DLC was allowed to charge a daily fee to pay for this service. It was what we were already doing with the kids for free, and now, I could bill a little over seventeen dollars for each day they attended. When multiplied by the number of children attending each day, this would add up to a sizable amount! It would not only help to pay for extra staff, it would also help buy supplies.

This was the first step into DLC becoming a legitimate program. We owe our future growth to Susan and remember her fondly. Sadly, she was taken too early by cancer and is honored each year by the Susan Jaskovich Award given to those making a difference in the lives of kids with special needs here in Jacksonville.

The next huge funder that helped us to financially stabilize was the United Way of North East Florida. I had reached out to them during our first year but was told that they had specific organizations that were approved by their board and were not accepting new applicants. They encouraged me by telling me how impressed they were by what the program was doing and acknowledged it was a real need in the community. I was disheartened but knew I was on to something. And I had learned how God worked on situations like this. Maybe, this was not the final word on the matter. Shortly after this negative call, the enrollment process opened to new groups, and a few months later, we were asked to apply again.

This time, DLC was accepted as a certified agency and got a check in the mail for twenty-five thousand dollars. I remember actually sitting down on the floor in shock. My wildest dreams for DLC had not foreseen anything like this coming. I didn't know this kind of funding was out there, but I sure knew what to do with it. So many more of our students had medical problems that really required a nurse's care. This is how I was able to offer our RN a part-time position with pay. I couldn't pay her what she was worth, but it gave her the amount she needed to get by. She was able to get paid for half a day's work and still volunteer for us part of the day. That was the sacrifice she chose to make so that the children were taken care of and healthy each day.

Applying for the United Way funding helped us to take another big step. We had to apply for our own tax-exempt number. Now, the school was a true not-for-profit program, and we were able to get our own nonprofit status with the state of Florida. We no longer had to use the tax-exempt code for the church; we had our very own certification and 501(c)(3) number. This was a big step for the school and for me. We were considered an official charity but still under the Murray Hill United Methodist Church. This would make grant money easier to obtain.

> For still the vision awaits its appointed time; it hastens to the end—it will not lie. If it seems slow, wait for it; it will surely come. (Habakkuk 2:3)

> Wait for the Lord; be strong, and let your heart take courage; wait for the Lord! (Psalm 27:14)

> But they who wait on the Lord shall renew their strength; they shall mount up with wings like eagles; they shall run and not be weary; they shall walk and not faint. (Isaiah 40:31)

Our growth was slow and steady over the next several years. We served about twelve to fifteen children each year. We expanded into three rooms of the church's Sunday-school building. In 1994, I was finally able to hire a full-time registered nurse, and that became a necessity when Jan moved out of state. With more medically involved students than ever before, a registered nurse's presence was needed the majority of the school day. Our new nurse, Mina, was a new nurse graduate. Once again, the timing was right as I heard about Mina graduating and looking for a job through family members. Just as we were ready to hire someone full-time, Mina became available. She was the sister of my sister-in-law. I think we both thought this was a temporary position for her, but she ended up working with me for over twenty-two years.

Miss Mina became an integral part of the school, even taking over our second location and making it a success after a rocky start. She was able to do nursing care at our primary location, now called DLC Nurse & Learn, in the morning and, then, go to our second location, DLC Therapy & Care, in the afternoon. Mina made sure all the children were cared for and healthy at both locations. She was another part of God's plan that came into DLC at just the right time—when she needed us, and we needed her.

During these years, we took on other part-time therapists. We now offered speech, occupational, and physical therapy, along with the developmental day training services and nursing care. But things were changing with the world of special-education services and not for the better.

Between 1989 and 1997, laws governing programming for children with disabilities were rapidly changing. Now that our kids finally had the right to an education, the government decided to get involved and control the funding and types of programming the kids received. I think much of the changes were intended for good, but as usual, the people making the rules aren't living by them and don't really understand the situation. A new way of thinking was taking over the special-education world. The term "natural environment" would come to haunt DLC. The idea was a sound one. The intent was to make sure that children with different developmental needs were not separated from other children. The new law meant that all children should learn together and not be placed in programs that were only for children with disabilities. This meant that programs like DLC were no longer considered appropriate and, therefore, should not receive funding. Our children, it was recommended, should be allowed to attend regular childcare programs or should be taught at home. Home was considered the only real natural environment. Some parents told me that they had been made to feel guilty for working away from the home because their children would get better care there with a therapist coming in one time a week to help out. I think this was a misinterpretation of the intent of the law. This was going against everything DLC stood for and was trying to accomplish for children and families. Of course, saving money is usually behind every decision the government makes about children with disabilities.

Also, a new government program called the Preschool Assistance Program (PAP) now was the source of all funding, and we had to be approved through this new program to receive the developmental day training dollars (DDT). We had been able to get paid for five days a week of DDT. The PAP program would only allow one to three days of DDT. It would get worse—much worse. Over time, this payment for our training service was cut back to all children, regardless of the severity of disability, only being allowed one day of DDT services. It was now changing to a specialized therapy service. All of these changes were supposed to be an improvement for kids, but I saw it as a way to cut dollars from kids that needed it most.

It was decided by the Preschool Assistance Program that we were not a natural environment as we only had children there with disabilities, so our funding was being gradually cut off, and no new children were being referred to us. As we always did, we learned to adapt. I realized that if we were going to be able to continue helping these children I loved, my program would have to change.

The tide was also changing with what was considered a natural environment. Since other children attend preschool, preschool was now considered a natural environment. But it was only natural if children attended that were developing along a typical path and pace. We began accepting children in the program that had no developmental delays. These children were considered "typically developing," and this became a new term for us. If we added these typical kids to the mix, we hoped DLC would get back in the good graces of the Preschool Assistance Program so we could get back to helping the families that needed us.

We had a new family come to visit with a two-year-old named August. He had severe cerebral palsy due to a problem that occurred during his birth. They moved here from California where all children were put in natural environments, and he was the only child in his class with a disability. However, no one in the school knew how to help August. His parents were a bit apprehensive about DLC but decided to give it a try. Within weeks, they were amazed at how we treated August. In his old school, they handled him and treated him like a baby. We talked to him like a two-year-old and had him sitting up to eat, not in our arms like an infant. They started to realize that we were expecting more out of him and giving him opportunities to do more two-year-old activities, not just put him in a room of two-year-olds. We worked at carrying him more upright and worked on seating that allowed him to be at the table with the other children. These are things most preschool teachers wouldn't know how to do, but the teachers at DLC did this sort of thing regularly.

August's parents even pointed out that in California, things were starting to shift, and more "center-based programs" were coming back, and children with more extreme delays were in classrooms that could serve them better. It was becoming clear that simply having children with delays around typically developing children and giving them weekly therapy wasn't enough. Trained teachers have to be involved on a daily basis, along with a staff that is experienced with all types of children with delays. This way, kids got the most out of each school day.

It would be a while before Florida caught up to the thinking that center-based programs were natural environments. The fact that DLC had some typically developing children enrolled helped, and eventually, the PAP program began to accept us and refer children to us again. However, there was now another twist. There was no longer developmental day training money available. Now, they only paid for one hour a week for early intervention service. This meant I had to get a new license to do what I had been doing for fifteen years as a special-education teacher with a bachelor's degree.

I had to take online classes to assure everyone that I knew how to work with children from birth to three years of age. I put in one hundred seventy hours reading early intervention information and taking online tests to get a new title. I was now an infant and toddler developmental specialist and could now earn the one-hour-a-week funds that we used to get paid five days a week to do. It was a lot of work, but this title allowed for funding that helped cover the costs of the program that I knew parents couldn't afford. This was one more step in making sure children were getting the training they needed and parents were able to afford our services so they could get and keep full-time jobs.

It seemed like things were never simple. Every time things started to look up for our funding, something would change to take other funding away. It was a constant battle to keep things running and to keep the negative forces from destroying what we had created for good. I guess that is why God made me stubborn. I refused to quit when a problem came up, I knew there was a solution out there; I simply had to get creative and find it.

> Therefore, since we are surrounded by so great
> a cloud of witnesses, let us also lay aside every
> weight and sin which clings so closely, and let us
> run with endurance the race that is set before us.
> (Hebrews 12:1)

More and more regulations and less allowable services and therapy have continued to restrict our program. Health insurance has become a nightmare for us and the families with constant changes and confusion, along with denials of basic therapy services so that payments are few and far between. We gradually were cut off from the Preschool Assistance Program completely. Once again, intentions may have been for good, but new ways of looking at services to save dollars made us out of compliance with the new therapy philosophy they were insisting we follow. Parents were asked to accept one therapy service at a time. They had to choose which therapy would be the most valuable with a "less is more" mentality. As our contract stated, we had to agree with this philosophy, and I did not.

We were told by their staff at the time that if parents complained about only being allowed one therapy service at a time, we had to side with PAP. We were told to quote their philosophy as if we really believed it was best. I just couldn't do that. We even explained to them that DLC had grant dollars to cover the extra therapy and that PAP would not have to pay for it. That was not acceptable to them because it made it appear we did not concur with the evaluation of their staff that a child only needed one therapy at a time.

I believe the children were not being put first, and lack of funding for these programs means even less services for kids. We know that if children are given opportunities every day in a stimulating environment, they will get better and reach their potential. While the brain is doing most of its growth between birth and three, we should be doing all the therapy needed to give children the best chance to rewire the brain. That was and is the only philosophy I will stand up for.

DLC became a full-inclusion program in 2003 and have been serving children with and without disabilities in a quality learning environment ever since. We are doing what we feel is the best practice for children with special needs, regardless of what the government agencies are doing or what they say is best.

Our change to full inclusion happened quite by chance as the Murray Hill Preschool, also housed in the same building as DLC, had decided to close their doors. This was another opportunity that God gave us to grow. We offered to take over the space and have our children in the classrooms alongside the Murray Hill Preschool children that wanted to stay. We needed the space to grow, and the students from the preschool needed a program. We already had all the training and licensing that the Murray Hill Preschool was lacking. New licensing requirements were not easy to meet, but we had already met them easily with more college-educated staff. We already met most of the requirements that day-care licensing now required and surpassed it with many of our staff having college degrees.

The church voted its approval, and the first full "inclusion" preschool in Jacksonville, Florida, was formed. It was not as easy as it sounds. This change was a struggle, at first, for our teachers, as they were not used to children that were always up and running around. We were not sure how to make this work. With a child on the floor unable to sit up and a child running around the room that might step on the child on the floor and injure them, it didn't seem to make sense. Also, how could we give the child with delays the same lessons as the child that was on a typical path of development for a three-year-old? Could we give them equal amounts of attention and not cheat one or the other out of quality-learning time? It was overwhelming to all of us, at first, but it became a blessing as the children each learned lessons from each other.

Our teachers gradually learned ways to juggle and blend all levels of learning. It gave our teachers another creative outlet, and soon, the classrooms took on a new look as the children with delays were encouraged to move and talk more. Now, it is often difficult at first glance to tell which children have developmental difficulties. Natural environment and DLC finally found common ground.

Many families prefer DLC for their children that are typically developing. Even if a child has no delay, they get the same individualized attention and learn even faster. One of the amazing things that has happened as a result of inclusion is that many children have been diagnosed that would have, otherwise, fallen through the cracks. Children now come in with less obvious delays that have not been diagnosed and, with our teachers and other trained staff, are quickly screened when delays become apparent. Then, we are able to start treatment much faster to get them back on track! With the ability to pick up on development problems, more children can catch up to their appropriate age level before they enter public school. Many of these children might have been overlooked in the past and would have started kindergarten, never having any intervention. Children that have not had the same opportunity for intervention start off behind and fall even further behind before action is taken in the larger school system.

Another surprise benefit is that children at a higher level automatically help those functioning with developmental challenges. If a child needs help raising their hand in circle time, the child sitting next to him will reach over and help put their friend's hand in the air. It becomes second nature to the children that are typically developing to become mentors to the kids with special needs. At this age, no bullying takes place. No toddler thinks about making fun of his friend. They don't even realize there is a difference. The situation is just considered a chance to help a friend that needs help. When one child helps another succeed, their self-esteem is increased, so it's a win-win situation.

These perks were never my intent, but they were obviously part of God's perfect plan. I have learned to go with the flow! When new things are happening and changing around me, I no longer panic or try and fight it. At least, not as much. Those changes and difficulties are usually God at work. I have now come to realize when something happens out of my control, it's best to trust the process and let God work out the details. His miracles, big and small, usually happen when changes come that we want to fight but can't.

> "My thoughts are not your thoughts and My ways are not your ways," declares the Lord. (Isaiah 55:8)

> For there is a time and a way for everything, although man's trouble lies heavy on him. (Ecclesiastes 8:6)

The other benefit is that the children without delays are learning lessons that can't be taught elsewhere. They are learning understanding and acceptance of differences that many adults fear. Children that have attended DLC will be comfortable all their lives with others that may have a disability or those differently abled. If children all got that lesson early in life, maybe, bullying would be a thing of the past. Many parents tell us that once their child leaves DLC and goes to kindergarten, teachers all comment on how patient the children are and how much more willing they are to wait their turn and pay attention to activities longer. I think these are all fringe benefits to being around children with developmental differences. We always say the children with disabilities are here to teach us, and in this case, it couldn't be more true.

> Only take care and keep your soul diligently lest you forget the things that your eyes have seen, and lest they depart from your heart all the days of your life. Make them known to your children and your children's children. (Deuteronomy 4:9)

Kimberly with me and her mom as pictured in the newspaper article

Kimberly with her cake from her 4<sup>th</sup> birthday party

Kimberly with her birthday doll gift

August at DLC with an adaptive toy

August with his family

August smiling while listening to his favorite music

# Chapter 6

## *God the Conductor*

*My mouth will tell of Your righteous acts, of Your deeds of salvation all the day, for their number is past my knowledge. With the mighty deeds of the Lord God I will come; I will remind them of Your righteousness, Yours alone. Oh God, from my youth You have taught me, and I still proclaim Your wondrous deeds. So even to old age and grey hairs, oh God, do not forsake me, until I proclaim Your might to another generation, Your power to those to come.*

—Psalms 71:15–18

*Great is our Lord, and abundant in power; His understanding is beyond measure.*

—Psalm 147:5

DLC was being forced to change in so many ways. More funding and growth began about the same time. God was ready to make His move! When God is making a big move, it is impossible to miss Him. Things started happening so fast that I didn't have time to second-guess my decisions. That was probably a good thing. People began to show up at the right place and time. More of those sneaky coincidences were happening all around me. Many happened at very unlikely places.

The Jaguars Foundation had been formed since the start of our NFL team in Jacksonville in 1995. It supported charity work in our city that focused on "at risk" children and teens. I had written grant proposals to them a couple of times over the years, but we had been turned down every time. We didn't quite fit their mold, but let's face it, DLC doesn't fit very many molds. We needed someone within the organization that would see the importance of what DLC was doing. The problem was I didn't know anyone on the inside and had very few contacts that were close to professional football. So I had quit writing grants to them, assuming it was never going to happen.

My son, Caleb, was born in December of '92. Yes, with no health insurance, and everything was paid for out of pocket. It can be done! At least, in 1992, it could be done. As a family of tennis fans, he had grown up watching the tennis greats and the excitement of the courts. He really enjoyed watching tennis on TV with me and wanted to learn how to play. We found tennis lessons were available in our neighborhood at Boone Park. One day, while he was taking lessons, a gentleman was there with his daughter who was also there for lessons. We struck up a conversation, and he asked what I did for a living. I explained what DLC Nurse & Learn was all about and our mission. He asked had we ever tried to get funds from the Jaguars Foundation, as he was, Peter Racine, the new president of the organization. Once the shock wore off, I told him that I had tried without success for years and never had been approved for funding. He told me to call him on Monday to talk about the next funding cycle.

That year, we received funding and continued to receive funding for the next ten years. The best part was the funds were to be used on staff, and that was our biggest need. Over the years, we received close to three hundred thousand dollars from the Jaguars Foundation, as well as funds for adaptive playgrounds at both locations and adaptive tricycles.

That was not the only connection God made for me. About that same time, I got a call from an old contact from many years ago. It felt more like a lifetime ago. Dorcas Tanner was the director of the United Cerebral Palsy program where I had volunteered every summer. She had become the director shortly after I started there and was the director there for many years after I left for college. Dorcas had retired by this time but was still active in the nonprofit community. She was aware of my special childcare and was looking for an agency to take over an after-school enrichment program for students with special needs. The program was now being run by Easter Seals, and they were leaving Jacksonville. It was also being housed at Mt. Herman, my old public school. Dorcas had just become interim director of Jacksonville Children's Commission, and they were starting the bidding process for a grant to take over the after-school program at Mt. Herman. We put in a bid for the opportunity to run it and got the grant for $225,000 to take care of thirty-five to forty students with disabilities after school. This was something we were already doing but with only ten to twelve children in our limited space.

There was one catch; we needed to find another place to house the extra children. The program that was now at Mt. Herman and the public-school system wouldn't allow the improvements we wanted to make. We wanted to do therapy with the children and have them stay longer. This would not work in the public-school building. Even though they had all the therapy equipment we needed, they were worried about us using it and damaging it, as we were not part of the public school. Also, the location was not ideal for parents to come pick up children later in the day as it was in a high crime district. The biggest issue was that the children were currently being transported home on school buses at an exorbitant rate that came out of the grant funds. We wanted to use that money for more staff and better programming. With the time it took to get them all home in the afternoon, the kids were picked up by 4:30 p.m. to ride home on the busses. This left no time for real learning to take place. The kids ate snacks, were changed, and then put back in wheelchairs and sat in front of toys at tables. By then, it was time for them to leave. There was simply not time for any therapeutic activities or one-on-one skills work.

Where in the world would we find a building big enough to house another twenty-five or more children and all the therapy equipment too? Our current location was pretty much maxed out already. I had absolutely no idea where to start looking. Well, God knew! He had been preparing a place already.

The Lakeshore Presbyterian Church had just closed their childcare center that had been there for many years and were heartbroken about it. The childcare building that had been full of children just six months before was sitting empty. They had seven rooms still full of furniture and toys. These seven classrooms just seemed to be waiting for us. While empty for six months, the rooms had begun to deteriorate and grow stinky with mildew. The church members really needed to get something in that space quickly and get it fixed up and running. But the church didn't have the money to make all the repairs needed. One of our past board members heard about it and about our need for more space and called up some old friends from the Lakeshore church. A group of elders from the church came and toured DLC and fell in love with the idea of us using the empty space for our special children. One of them said, "This isn't just a day care, this is a *real* ministry." We all knew this was another match made in heaven.

With the new funding and new space, DLC Therapy & Care was born in October of 2003. The Children's Commission even allowed us to use some of the funds to fix up the deteriorating classrooms. We did a major clean up, put fresh paint on the walls, installed new tile on the floors, and bought all-new therapy equipment for a state-of-the-art therapy room!

We struggled, at first, to find an appropriate nurse that met our standards. We had some initial staff come and go. We needed someone we could trust to have another quality program. Our first full-time registered nurse, Mina Geisel, rejoined our staff after a two-year detour with another company. While away, she had gained just the right skills needed to take on more leadership at DLC and took on the dual role of head nurse and program director for the therapy and care after-school program.

We were now able to care for up to forty after-school children, rather than the ten to twelve we were helping before. Eventually, this also turned into a full summer camp for our school-age kids with an extra fifty thousand dollars in funding from Jacksonville Children's Commission. This way, when public school was out for the summer, our students would have continuation of services and therapy so that skills would not be lost over the summer break. This has been very valuable to our families as summer-school services in the public schools have been reduced to only a few short weeks in the summer for children with severe disabilities and cut completely for most. The last several years, most children we serve don't even qualify for the few weeks available. All of these families would have stopped working over the summer and lost jobs, so summer camp was crucial to parents as well as kids.

These changes to my little program all took place is a span of two years. It was not so little anymore. After 2003, things had been steadily improving for DLC, financially. There had also been a steady increase in the number of students whose families heard about DLC and needed our care. And more families were finding out about how the program at DLC took even severely delayed children. They now realized that childcare was possible for children like theirs. A waiting list was always very long for families needing our services, and once our after-school program filled to capacity, it was next to impossible to get a space. Families can stay in the after-school programs until their child is twenty-two years, and they graduate high school. As long as we had the funds to cover the tuition, the kids just kept coming, and the waiting list just kept growing.

With the addition of the new Murray Hill Preschool rooms and the new rooms at Lakeshore Presbyterian, we had more space than ever, but DLC was almost always full. We had fifty students at the first location and, at least, another twenty at the new building. It was hard for me to believe that a few short years before, we were running a program in two rooms with an average of just ten to fifteen total children.

If I had stopped to think for very long, I would have panicked. We had gone from a handful of employees and a budget of just over one hundred thousand dollars to almost thirty employees and a budget that was getting closer to one million dollars. I thought God would keep growing us.

I began looking for more dollars and more space, waiting for God to make another big move. After twenty years, DLC did start getting recognition and several awards. We were given the Gifts of Service Award from the Child Development Education Alliance two times. We won a Sapphire award from Florida Blue Foundation twice as a Sapphire honoree along with $75,000. That was after an original $99,000 grant from Florida Blue Foundation a few years before. I was even recognized for my life's work with an award from the Sherwood Smith Foundation. I was also extremely honored to be a finalist and runner up for the Eve Award. The nomination came from a ladies group at Mandarin United Methodist. The Eve Award recognizes women that have made a difference in city of Jacksonville and is a pretty big deal around these parts. I remember thinking things were going to explode for DLC after the Eve Award gave so much press to my little school. This, unfortunately, didn't happen.

DLC did get some big grants, and other donations kept rolling in. However, with grants comes more demands as well. As fast as money came in, it was spent on a larger staff and costs of operating a larger program. Our budget grew, and I assumed a third DLC was in God's plans, but that did not happen either. It seemed like the perfect next step to put another DLC facility on the south side so families from the other side of Jacksonville and Jax Beach could access us more easily. Jacksonville is a huge city—very spread out. Actually, its land mass is the biggest in the United States. So my plan, and I was sure it was God's plan too, was to open another DLC as soon as possible.

I reached out to several possible churches and other building possibilities, thinking it would be God's next move. But I was obviously wrong. The next thing to happen was almost a complete collapse of the whole program. Was that God too? After all the times God had helped to make DLC happen and then to grow, would He just let everything fail?

After huge accolades and several big grants, I felt all our financial worries were a thing of the past. We were finally building an emergency fund and had over eighty thousand dollars saved up. Our new district superintendent for the NE district advised me to take some time off. I took his advice and took the summer of 2010 off, only going in to work with kids once a week and to take care of emergencies. I actually started writing this book, and things seemed to be going fine. Staff handled everything well; the program ran like clockwork without me. I actually felt a little hurt that, maybe, I wasn't needed anymore. But I liked the feeling knowing that if something happened to me, DLC would go on. When I got back to work that August, the reality set in. Funding and donations had both slowed down. Medicaid and insurance payments for therapy had shrunk drastically due to changes in Medicaid.

The worst part was that the downturn in the economy had hit us hard in every area, including enrollment. If parents couldn't find jobs, they didn't need day care. One of the ways we brought in income was by charging the families with typically developing children a full childcare rate. This helped subsidize the scholarship fund for low-income families. Many of the parents were looking for work because previous employment had been lost after the birth of their medically fragile child. Unable to balance work and their child's condition, which is often too time consuming, many parents gave up successful careers. Parents with healthy children could pay for full tuition but, now, no longer could afford it, and we had almost nothing coming in to maintain a scholarship fund. We took the painful approach of cutting scholarships. This shrunk class sizes and therapy needs which meant staff needed to shrink too. As I had done in the past, I went without pay for several months, and many staff worked for less pay, less hours, and many were let go or quit. It was the darkest time for DLC ever, and I really had no answers to the problems. Usually, God had come through in some big miracle that was out of the blue. I kept waiting for that to happen, but it didn't this time.

I had wrestled, many times, with my faith and had always been right to trust God and His timing. I even had learned the lesson that if God was in the middle of DLC, then, I had to trust Him more than myself and more than DLC. God was the reason I was doing what I was doing; He was my focus, not the ministry. I had learned long ago that if the ministry ended, I would be all right. I wasn't

DLC, and God wasn't DLC; it was just part of God's plan for my life. This time, I really thought His plan for my life was changing, and I trusted that if we closed the doors to DLC, it just meant God would start a new chapter. Even though I had faith, it didn't feel good not knowing. Nobody likes the unknown in their future. This seemed very much like the "valley of the shadow of death" talked about in Psalms. The one thing I did know was that God was in control, and I tried to convince myself that if He was leading it, then, things would turn out all right. I still had a nagging guilt that I had messed up somewhere.

> For in Him we live and move and have our being. As some of your poets have said, "We are His offspring." (Acts 17:28)

> But none of these things move me, neither count I my life dear unto myself, so that I might finish my course with joy, and the ministry, which I have received of the Lord Jesus, to testify the gospel of the grace of God. (Acts 20:24)

> Even though I walk through the darkest valley, I will fear no evil, for You are with me; Your rod and Your staff, they comfort me. (Psalm 23:4)

Bible study became breathing to me and prayer like a transfusion of hope. God spoke to me often when I became silent during a prayer time. I don't mean a voice, but ideas would come that I knew, in my heart, were not from me but from Him.

Ideas would pop into my mind out of nowhere, and these thoughts were not anything like my thoughts.

But one day, after praying and while I was being quiet and just listening, God really spoke. I heard an audible voice. Now, skeptics will say that I may have fallen asleep and dreamed it, or my mind was playing tricks. I even thought that myself, at first.

The strangest part was the voice itself. Even believers will expect me to describe a deep, strong, booming voice that gave me the perfect answer for how to turn things around quickly and save DLC. But it wasn't anything like that. It wasn't overwhelming or fancy or mind-blowing. You might say it was a "still small voice" of wisdom.

I heard an audible voice that said, "Keep moving forward." The silliest part is that it sounded like one of The Beatles; Ringo Star, I think. I know you are probably laughing. It's all right; at the time, I did too. But those three words gave me the reassurance that I didn't need to do anything grand like writing a million-dollar grant or anything drastic like shutting down and calling it quits. It made me realize that if I started DLC from nothing twenty years earlier, I could do it again, and with a good reputation and a little more knowledge, it would be easier this time around. The answers to our biggest problems might not be miracles. Maybe just "keeping going" and not giving up is the miracle.

> And he said, Go forth, and stand upon the
> mount before the Lord, and behold, the Lord

passed by, and a great wind rent the mountains, and broke in pieces the rocks before the Lord; but the Lord was not in the wind. And after the wind an earthquake; but the Lord was not in the earthquake. And after the earthquake a fire; but the Lord was not in the fire. And after the fire a still small voice. (1 Kings 19:11–12)

And let us not grow weary of doing good, for in due season we will reap, if we do not give up. (Galatians 6:9)

I can do all things through Him who strengthens me. (Philippians 4:13)

But you, take courage! Do not let your hands be weak, for your work shall be rewarded. (2 Chronicles 15:7)

Fear not, for I am with you; be not dismayed, for I am your God; I will strengthen you, I will help you, I will uphold you with My righteous right hand. (Isaiah 41:10)

Therefore, having this ministry by the mercy of God, we do not lose heart. (2 Corinthians 4:1)

There are so many verses about trusting in God and not giving into fear because life can be hard to navigate. It's impossible without faith. Faith gives us the strength to carry on in the face of overwhelming odds. That was the big question; after twenty-plus years, did I have the strength, the energy, the determination to keep going?

For over twenty years, I had fought for DLC, working way too many hours, and I didn't know if I had enough fight left in me. It might just be easier to move on to a nine-to-five job where I just get my paycheck and go home. If I had stayed at my teaching job in public school, I would be making more money, have more time off, and none of this pressure. But I also knew that life wasn't for me.

My love for the kids and families we help was just as strong; I knew that. The need they have is just as great. I thought about all the kids we had helped over the years. The success stories that were true miracles. The success stories over the years were all the proof I needed that I had to keep going—keep *moving forward*. Neither the kids nor their parents can give up, so I knew we couldn't either. The thing that inspired me to start DLC and to keep going were the amazing kids, their hero parents, and the many miracle stories I have witnessed. I would like to share some of them with you in the next chapter.

> This service that you perform is not only supplying the needs of the Lord's people but is also overflowing in many expressions of thanks to God. (2 Corinthians 9:12)

Let us hold fast to the confession of our hope without wavering, for he who promised is faithful. (Hebrews 10:23)

Be strong and courageous. Do not be afraid for the Lord your God goes with you, He will never leave you or forsake you. (Deuteronomy 31:6)

Zachary with baby brother Caleb

Me and my two boys

# CHAPTER 7

# *Worth Fighting For*

*Because of the service by which you have proved yourselves, others will praise God for the obedience that accompanies your confession of the gospel of Christ, and for your generosity in sharing with them and with everyone else. And in their prayers for you their hearts will go out to you. Thanks be to God for His incredible gifts.*

—(2 Corinthians 9:13–15)

The obvious reason to fight for DLC to stay open was the kids. Over the years, there have been some pretty amazing stories; I call them miracles. So many students with so many amazing stories that I could never begin to tell about them all. I will share some of the most amazing stories and not all had nicely wrapped up endings but are just as miraculous as the ones that did. As a church program, we prayed for our students on a regular basis. Many times, I would tell the parents that since we are connected to a church, we are a school that is allowed to pray. This is something we did as a staff but also had many other churches and individuals praying for specific children and their needs all over northeast Florida. The following stories are the results.

*Simon*

One of the first and, maybe, most incredible DLC stories is that of Simon. When he first visited DLC with his mom, Laura, Simon was a seven-month-old baby with many birth defects. He was missing one eye, had only one ear that didn't work so well, and had webbed fingers and toes. He had been diagnosed with lissencephaly, which means smooth brain. Generally, children with this disorder don't have the usual folds and bumps you see in pictures of an average developed brain. This is a degenerative condition, and children generally lose skills over time and pass away before the age of two.

The worst part is that Simon came with a DNR or "do not resuscitate" order. This meant if Simon stopped breathing and his heart stopped beating, we could not do CPR. The only action allowed was to call 911 and let the paramedics take him and pronounce him deceased when the inevitable happened. I later found out that his mom said she was strong armed into signing this order. She was young, and they told her she had no choice; it was not what she wanted.

The school staff were all shocked at first, but we would have many more DNR orders come in attached to children over the years. This was a thin sheet of paper that held much weight! Our response was simple; just put it in the file and let God take care of it.

Simon was, however, one of the cutest kids we had ever seen, and his mom was going to college during the morning and needed someone to watch him. She had waited seven months, thinking he wasn't going to live, so she stayed at home with him, wanting to stay with him every minute. After time passed, she realized he might actually live, so she should start living again too.

We decided to write goals for him and work with him just like our other students. He received therapy services, and we began to see progress. He went from sitting to crawling, just a little late, and was playing with toys and making some sounds. By the end of his first year, he seemed to be catching up, but we reasoned the brain has not started the downward cycle yet.

He went for his first checkup in Miami where specialists were for children born with lissencephaly. The doctors were stunned that the folds had started to develop in Simon's brain. He no longer had a smooth brain. The second year, Simon started to walk and talk and was beginning to learn his body parts and the names of animals. He got surgery to separate his fingers and toes and received occupational therapy at DLC so he could learn to color, dress himself, and use a spoon. After his second checkup with the specialists, they declared his brain had developed to within normal limits!

Upon graduation from DLC at age three, Simon was just a little behind other three-year-olds in development. He could count to ten, knew his colors, and could even recognize his first name. He attended special classes in public school and continued to improve. By first grade, he was placed in a regular first-grade classroom. At the end of his first-grade year, he was reading at the top of his class and playing baseball after school. His mom, Laura, had also graduated from college with a degree in business.

At our twentieth anniversary, Simon was the most popular speaker of the night. He took my microphone and proceeded to tell the audience about his many accomplishments and even did a karate demonstration to show what he had learned in karate class. His mom has now gone back to school to get a speech-therapy degree. When he became a teenager, Simon even came to volunteer with us to help out during summer camp. Talk about paying it forward!

Simon has now graduated high school a year early with a dual enrollment in college, so he will be starting college with an associate of arts degree. They still visit DLC to keep us updated so we continue to be amazed at the young man that ignored the doctor's diagnoses and was one of our first DLC miracles.

*Stephen*

Stephen is another student that was, and still is, a part of the DLC family! He and I are friends on Facebook, and we stay in touch. He has come so far, and I couldn't help but share his amazing story with you. His accomplishments continue to warm our hearts, and it's because of students like Stephen that I couldn't let DLC close. Stephen is a young man with cerebral palsy and started DLC pre-school at two years of age. He was being raised by his grandmother, and they had a special bond. She was working, and Stephen attended full-time at DLC and then after-school once he started public school at age four.

His physical therapy sessions often ended in a wrestling match with my brother, Marc, our physical therapist at the time. After a long session of stretching his muscles and tendons, which Stephen hated, he would always beg Marc to wrestle with him for fun. This was a reward, but many times, Marc found fun ways to incorporate more therapy into the wrestling match. Stephen was very smart, but communication was difficult for him due to poor breath control from tight/weak chest muscles. Hours of speech therapy and breathing exercises paid off, and he was able to attend regular high school. He was still in a wheelchair, but with the help of an assistant to help him get around and take notes for him, he was quite successful.

He has become a writer and a poet and attended our twentieth anniversary as well, reading one of his poems to the audience. There was not a dry eye in the room. He not only wrote a moving, insightful poem, but read it to a room full of people with elegance and poise. As he sat in his wheelchair, holding the microphone, I was astonished at the accomplished young man he had become. His wheelchair had not diminished his desire to succeed or his passion for life.

Stephen graduated from Trinity Christian Academy, interestingly enough, alongside my youngest son, Caleb. He moved back home with his father for a short time, after the passing of his grandmother. Losing her was the hardest thing he has faced. He is now in community college in Georgia and living independently in a special assisted-living residence! We are so proud of how far Stephen has come, and we know his future will be filled with even more accomplishments.

*Trevon*

Children are oftentimes the best teachers, and that can truly be said of one of my first students. Trevon was, as they say, an old soul. He was born with the most severe form of arthrogryposis. This congenital defect halts the development of certain muscles and joints. In most children that are born with it, only the arms and wrists are affected, but in the most severe cases, hips, legs, and ankles are underdeveloped as well. In Trevon's case, his face and jaw were also involved. This left him unable to chew well or even to smile. At least, that's what we thought until we got to know him. He had a way of smiling that that made everyone fall in love with him. It took so much effort for him to make his face smile, but he knew how a smile looked, and he would do his best to make his muscles go into a smile shape. It wasn't like a regular smile but, somehow, even better. He was G-tube fed because he couldn't chew and swallow enough to give him proper nutrition, so like many of our students, he needed nursing care.

His mom was single and in the military and needed DLC so he could come during the hours she was at the military base here in Jacksonville. She also was deployed for six months at a time, and he would stay with Grandma until Mom returned. DLC was the only answer for this amazing family that served our country while dealing with so many issues.

Nothing seemed to get them down. Trevon and his mom were always positive. What amazed me the most about the incredible young boy was his creative mind. He couldn't use his arms except to swing them from his shoulders and have them flop onto a toy. His wrists were curled, so his hands folded back useless, for the most part. If placed in a chair, he could sit but easily could fall out, due to lack of hip stability, and of course, walking was out of the question. He could scoot around at a rapid rate on the floor and got to where he wanted to go without a problem.

He wanted to sit at the table with the other children, so we learned to strap him in a chair to keep him from falling out. He would point with his head since his arms couldn't lift up to do so. He would look at what he wanted and bop his head down and up to show us his intended toy. One day, he "pointed" to a toy that had beads on a wire to play with. This required arm, hand, and fine motor skills that he didn't possess. I offered other toys that were more appropriate, but he insisted on the bead toy. I put him in the chair at the table and placed the toy in front of him on the table. I put a rubber mat under it to prevent him from knocking it off. He swung his arm up and was able to hit the toy but couldn't play with it. Or so I thought. I figured he would realize that it was no fun and give up. But actually, he had a plan that I was not privy to. He put his hand on the base of the toy to stabilize it and, then, leaned forward. He bent his head down and put his forehead on a bead and, then, moved it up and down on the wire. I was blown away! He had a ball moving each bead around the wire track. This was not the way the manufacturers intended the toy to be used but it worked. I was taught a lesson that day. The teacher had been taught! Give a child opportunity, and they will learn. Maybe not the conventional way, maybe in their own way, but they will find a way. Trevon taught me to be more creative in my lesson plans and work until a way is found for every child to be a success.

*Brandon*

Brandon started DLC Nurse & Learn with his sister, Brandi, in 1998, when they were both one-year-olds. He and Brandi are twins born prematurely, and as often happens, he lost oxygen at birth. This happens many times with the second twin that is delivered, if the birth takes too long. Brandi had speech delays but caught up quickly to her peers. Brandon was not as fortunate and has severe spastic cerebral palsy and couldn't walk or even sit up on his own. However, Brandon always seemed so intelligent, and the sounds he made sounded like words every once in a while. We encouraged his "yes and no" response to questions, and he began to tell us how old he was when asked. He even started saying three- and four-word sentences. It was so exciting to hear his sweet little voice telling us all the thoughts that have been bottled up in his head for so long.

Brandon now loves to talk and lights up the room everywhere he goes with his kindness and laughter. He would only eat hotdogs for the longest time, and now enjoys eating almost everything, and even asks the staff, "What's for dinner?" from time to time. As soon as anyone meets Brandon, he now has a new best friend. They always want to drop by to see him, and no matter where I go, people have heard about him and want to know how he is doing.

Brandon is the closest thing we have to a true DLC celebrity. When we share his picture on Facebook in one of our online stories, he gets the most comments from his devoted fanbase. His speaking improvements have continued through high school. So much so that he even said the *entire* pledge of allegiance by himself at the Mt. Herman Graduation in 2014. Brandon has now graduated himself at eighteen but continues at Mt. Herman through the special public-school program to help graduates reach more independence up to age twenty-two.

It's hard to believe that a human being can radiate so much love and joy while strapped in a wheelchair. He has never accomplished any academic goals or won any awards for great sports achievements. Brandon can't even care for himself and needs help with all of his daily needs, yet no one on Earth brings more fun and laughter to a room. If awards could be given for powerful personalities, Brandon would get first prize.

He also loves going to church and singing hymns and gospel music and wants to be a preacher one day. His favorite phrase is, "Praise the Lord," said at a very fast pace. We even got him on video, singing and praising the Lord and shared it in my home church. With the personality and joy he has, he would really make a good preacher. And actually, is a preacher already in the real sense of the word. All things are possible, after all!

*Kiara*

Then, there was Kiara! I smile just thinking about this spunky, sassy, stubborn girl. When Kiara's grandmother first brought her to visit, she was frail and unresponsive. Grandma had just been given custody of seven-month-old Kiara, along with another young grand-child. Grandma was overwhelmed and scared. She wanted to find childcare for Kiara so she could keep her full-time job but knew her special granddaughter needed therapy during the day if she was ever going to overcome her severe disabilities. Kiara was born prematurely and had hydrocephalus and a shunt to drain the excessive fluid on her brain. The shunt was inserted to prevent further damage, but the presence of cerebral palsy was already apparent. Cerebral palsy can present itself in many forms. Some children are spastic and stiff, others have wild uncontrollable movements, while some children are limp like ragdolls. She was very floppy and weak and had almost no use of her left side. And Kiara's head was usually turned to one side. She was very much like a stroke victim.

DLC was the answer to grandma's prayers with all the therapies she needed at the day-care center, along with nursing care available for Kiara's medical problems. Therapy was started right away, and she received physical, occupational, and speech therapy weekly, along with the encouragement of our teachers that worked with her every day. The teachers followed up with therapy activities in the classroom to help her along, but results didn't happen right away. And they certainly didn't come easily.

Progress was very slow, at first. Kiara did a lot of sleeping and had several hospitalizations the first year. She didn't cooperate with therapy at all, even though the therapists took extra time convinc-ing her that therapy was fun! She was cute but obstinate and, many times, would appear to fall asleep during sessions. It didn't take long for us to realize she was faking it to get out of her therapy. Her physical limitations did not affect her intelligence. Her sneaky factor was fully intact. It made her even more endearing to all of us.

As Kiara grew, she learned to enjoy the extra attention she got from therapists. Still, her weak muscles and poor attention span hindered her development. Her left side was more affected and made crawling and playing with toys difficult. With our scholarship program, we were able to keep her in our full-day program, even when Grandma lost her day-care funding the state provided. This allowed the continuation of services Kiara needed to reach her full potential. We never gave up trying but were not sure if our hard work would pay off. Even I had my doubts about her potential. She just didn't progress the way I expected. Every advance she made was followed by regression from illness or from behavior issues.

Some children are just not on a direct path for success. Kiara was one of those children. Most children learn to walk first by having their hands held for support, but Miss Kiara didn't like her hands touched. She suddenly gained steam before she turned three, and her progress took off. Our physical therapist, Marc, realized she would take steps if holding onto a bar, and while holding on to the bar, she could be led around the room without fear of falling. She wouldn't let us hold her hands, but we could hold the bar without her complaining. Our occupational therapist, Carol, had started using the bar to make her use both hands, and thus, she overcame fears she had held onto that prevented her physical improvement. This was no fancy piece of equipment. The bar was a loose pole to teach grasping, which the therapists taped up and held out for her to grab. It was the right size, shape, and was lightweight, so the therapists could hold it for a long time while she walked around the school, even going up and down steps. The tape they used was bright-red, and she liked it. As long as it worked, it didn't matter how fancy it was. Much of the equipment for our students is unbelievably expensive, but sometimes, the simple, made-up therapy items worked just as well.

It was a miracle pole to us, and even though it didn't cost us much, it was a priceless tool for this child! At one point, her grandmother became frustrated at her slow progress. She brought in an article about a fancy piece of equipment that would strap her in and make her walk by moving her legs in a reciprocal motion. It looked like it would work wonders, and she insisted we should have equipment like this to work with the children. We, of course, couldn't afford it, but sometimes, fancy equipment isn't any better that human ingenuity. We had to explain that the pole actually was better because it made Kiara balance more, and she was doing more of the work herself. Grandma agreed and gave us more time to prove it.

At age three, she was talking, feeding herself, and walking independently! She was doing so well; she was able to walk down the aisle to accept her diploma as she graduated from DLC that summer. Her grandmother was no longer overwhelmed and scared. She was overwhelmed with how far Kiara had come, and we were, once again, amazed at the drastic change we saw in this child in such a short period of time. It will never become commonplace to see what can only be described as a miracle. These changes in children that can only be explained as works of God. Now, her grandma realized the future was going to be bright for her precious little girl.

*Jaylon*

Jaylon was about six months old when his parents brought him in for a tour of the DLC campus and to be evaluated. Jaylon's medical history was bleak and with severe brain bleeds at birth, according to his report. I have to admit I wasn't expecting much from this little guy. When his mom handed him to me so she could fill out our enrollment forms, I was quite surprised. When I read through the forms that were sent ahead, this little baby was described as devastated and fragile. I had envisioned a sickly infant with very little reaction to outside stimulus. I braced myself for a sad case with a mom that would have to accept her son might never improve much. Jaylon was predicted to be significantly vision-impaired, but his eyes connected with mine right away. He had fairly good head control and actually reached slightly toward a toy I held out for him. This responsive baby couldn't be the same one I read about in the paperwork.

Jaylon enrolled at DLC, and the surprises kept coming; Jaylon was a few months behind, at first, but quickly caught up to his age level with physical development. He loved his physical therapy and, by two, was not only walking but running on the playground. His vision was somewhat impaired, and he had to be reminded to look down when walking so he wouldn't trip over things and when going up and down steps. But the miracles were just a regular occurrence with Jaylon. By the time he was three years old, he was almost completely on age level physically, socially, and cognitively. He was talking in sentences, counting, and knew his colors even with the label of "legally blind." Jaylon's little sister attended DLC when she was born too, and they both were thriving when Mom moved and had to transfer them to another school. Jaylon enrolled in regular preschool and is still one of the most surprising miracles ever at DLC. He never seemed to understand how serious his medical problems were from birth and just ignored the prognosis that accompanied them. It is children like Jaylon that have taught us to ignore doctor's reports and wait on God's report. I still see this "legally blind" child running around the playground, kicking a ball. He had to work to see it, but he could. No one that saw him would have had a clue of his condition. We put red tape on the steps going upstairs so he could see the edge of each step, and that tape is still there, reminding us of Jaylon, the miracle boy.

*Andrew*

Another one of the biggest surprises I've had over the years is the story of Andrew. He is one of our students that has blossomed into a wonderful little boy, and he continues to make so much progress that every time I see him, he is a different kid. He is another one that just didn't seem to be progressing much at all at the beginning, but we just kept pushing him and hoping.

When Andrew first started DLC, he was less than a year old. Andrew couldn't do very much on his own. He usually could be found on the floor on his back, which was his preferred position and wanted to be left alone. He needed a lot of assistance in just sitting up, touching toys, playing with other students, and he couldn't speak or even make any noises. He stayed in one place unless he was moved by his teachers or therapists, but his teachers always felt Andrew was capable of much more with our help and his determination. The problem with Andrew was that he didn't seem to have any determination.

When sitting up for more than a few minutes, he would start crying like he was in pain. His torso was oddly shaped, and we really began to wonder if he would ever sit on his own. We feared that pushing him to try new positions might actually be causing him pain. We continued to push him with caution. This is a case that definitely was helped by our inclusion program at DLC. He saw the other children getting toys and wanted to get to them himself. Before leaving the toddler room, he was finally sitting up and beginning to scoot to toys a little. He even got up on his hands and knees and started to crawl a bit. We were all thrilled to see that he was finally showing some progress. At two and a half years of age, he was still significantly delayed and beginning to catch up to a typical six-month-old level.

Once he moved to the three-year-old class, he really took off. Watching the other big boys running around and playing really inspired him. His crying finally stopped altogether, as he was busy watching the other children and didn't have time for that anymore. He realized if he didn't work harder, he wouldn't be able to keep up with the other children, and he wanted that. I don't think any of us ever considered he would run around with them. We just hoped he could, at the very least, walk with assistance to get places. We thought that with a walker, he might be able to keep up with the others.

It is situations like this that show how valuable inclusion programs can be to students with even the most severe disabilities. His teacher really pushed him and treated him like one of her other three-year-olds. It all started to click for Andrew by age three. He began standing for a few minutes at a time, started eating more and trying to feed himself, even drink from an open cup. The big shift was his level of understanding and following directions. It was now obvious that Andrew was bright, and there was no stopping his progress once his teachers and therapists figured that out. I remember getting a call up in my office that I had to come see what Andrew was doing now. I headed down the stairs to see what was happening. Andrew had decided he wanted lunch and had pulled up to stand at the lunch table. He had even figured out how to get himself into the chair. His teacher said she wouldn't help him and had waited for him to do it by himself. The grin of success was on his face, and this was one proud little boy. This one-time event became a daily one. Andrew realized he was just one of the guys!

By the time Andrew was four years old, he had completely changed! He learned to play with his classmates, sit up, and stand on his own. He became much more verbal and started to say some words and even started taking steps with his hands held by an adult. He honestly didn't even look like the same child. The only thing that ever slowed him down were his seizures. He did battle a pretty severe seizure disorder, but thankfully, Andrew always bounced back quickly from each episode.

At the age of five, Andrews's big accomplishment was walking completely on his own. He started by using a walker, and then, he became very efficient walking with one hand held. By the time Andrew graduated to kindergarten, he was not only walking but running, dancing, and jumping. He was talking in phrases, following directions, and pretty much a regular kid; the kind of kid he always wanted to be. He may need some assistance to keep up in kindergarten, but he tested higher than some of the other typically developing children on his final voluntary prekindergarten exam. From a child that we thought would never sit alone to one that now we believe can make it in public school is truly a miracle. His mom once was unsure if she could take care of a little boy with so many delays. His dad jumped in and took over while she needed his support. She was afraid of not being strong enough to take care of him. Mom is now enjoying the little boy she nearly gave up on. This is a family success story as well.

*Kevin*

I can't tell about memorable students and not tell you about our Kevie. I still tear up at the thought of him. He was one of those miracle stories that didn't have a perfect ending, but I still consider him a miracle. A successful life can't always be measured in length of years. Kevin started out a typical little boy and progressed at an average rate until about three. He began stumbling and falling and lost bladder control at the age of four. His worried parents took him to the doctor and got the devastating news that Kevin had Tay-Sachs disease. Tay-Sachs is a degenerative genetic disorder that is from a recessive gene. In other words, a hidden monster. Its symptoms are caused by the lack of a certain enzyme that breaks down fatty lipids in the body, so they build up, gradually destroying the nervous system, the brain, and other organs. Most children with Tay-Sachs pass away by age eight, but not Kevie. He loved coming to DLC and being with the other children and, of course, got excellent nursing care from our RN, Miss Mina. He was the sweetest little guy and won over all of the staff with his grin and lovable spirit.

He gradually would require a tracheotomy to breath and gastronomy tube to eat. But he continued to live and be happy and enjoy his school time. His doctor was convinced that with the great care he got at DLC and because he had some place to look forward to going each day, it prolonged his life. Even when he couldn't play anymore, he had other children playing around him, keeping him motivated. There was music and laughter and plenty of love to keep him going.

Kevin finally passed away at the age of fifteen. His parents donated his trust fund to DLC, and many scholarships have been given over the years through this money to help many other children, but none more memorable than Kevin. He had such a wonderful sense of humor. I remember so many funny things about him. He always kept us laughing. One of the things that always made him laugh was diaper-changing time. He loved it when we changed his diaper and said he had a "tiny hiney!" He loved the rhyming words and always said it after us. Then, he would giggle uncontrollably. I can still hear his sweet voice repeating that silly phrase. We know he lives on in heaven, but he lives on in our memories as well.

*Caroline*

My very first student to enroll was Caroline, an adorable little baby with a big smile and round chubby face. Caroline was born with tuberous sclerosis (TS). TS is another fatal genetic disorder that her mom described as the "elephant man's disease on the inside." We have had many children come through DLC with TS since, but I had never heard of it until I met Caroline. She was our first student ever and first child with TS, and she taught me so much as a teacher. As my first student at DLC and, at the time, the only one that was full-time, I had lots of time to work with her. She had feeding disorders and was very orally defensive. I had found a speech therapist in the area, Katherine Towers, and I learned from her many of the techniques we still use today. I also learned, with trial and error, how to get Caroline to eat. I discovered that the same techniques that stimulated her to eat, often helped her with vocalizing too.

Caroline came so far in her short nine years. Eventually, the disease would take her from this Earth. This was one of the first children's funerals I ever attended. Her family were members of Evangel Temple in Jacksonville, and the pastor gave the best eulogy I've ever heard. He said that perhaps the reason Caroline was taken so soon is that she had fulfilled her life's purpose more quickly than most. She had brought more people to prayer in her short nine years than most ministers ever do. That meant so much to me and to her family and is probably very true. She was and is very loved.

*Brandon R*

No, this isn't a repeat story. We actually had two amazing students named Brandon attend DLC. They both have made a lasting impression on us. This Brandon story is a completely different story but, maybe, even more amazing than the first Brandon. His mother, Missy, told me the story over a sandwich at a local restaurant. Her first child, Adea, was perfect, and she never imagined she could have a child with special needs. She and her husband wanted more children and got pregnant right away with baby number two. Adea was only thirteen months old, but this was their plan. It was not their plan, however, to find out there were multiple problems at the first sonogram evaluation. Brandon was tiny—too tiny. There were many other red flags like placenta previa, and the amniocentesis showed a risk for spina bifida. They were referred to a specialty doctor for the remainder of the pregnancy. After more problems with the birth, they were told there was no chance the baby would live, and an abortion was recommended.

Missy and her husband, Paul, insisted on another sonogram. After seeing a heartbeat, they refused an abortion. Brandon was born on Valentine's day, and his mom considered this a sign that he was a gift from God. He was 1 pound 4 ounces at birth and 11 1/2 inches long. His ear was so small she remembered it look like a single rose petal. To her, he was perfect; tiny but *fearfully and wonderfully made*, she thought. Upon examination, it was found that Brandon was missing a wall in his heart, and blood was pumping into his lungs. The doctors told her that his problems were physical and couldn't be prayed away. This did not shake her faith. She and Paul kept praying, and three days later, a nurse let them know that his heart was completely healed. The doctor admitted that he didn't know who they knew, but Brandon was just fine. After six months, they were able to take home their perfect gift from God. Their church knew they needed help and gave them a vehicle to use to take him for therapy, but it was stolen. Missy believes this was God's plan as she found out about our services at DLC, and we were able to do in home therapy until they could bring him to us. They finally began bringing him to DLC when Adea began stuttering, and they felt she needed more attention. Siblings are often under stress that isn't recognized. Luckily, her parents did realize she needed some extra love, and they were able to give that to her while Brandon was at preschool.

We did full evaluations on Brandon, and his parents were brought in for a meeting to share our findings. They remember the day we told them that Brandon was developmentally delayed and possibly had autism. She said it was devastating, but we were able to counsel them and remind them that the labels didn't change anything, just gave us tools to be able to help him reach his potential.

And that is just what he did! Brandon has surpassed everyone's expectations. Once Mom and Dad decided to celebrate Brandon for who he was and simply look at all he could do, instead of focusing on what he couldn't do, they realized he was truly a treasure. He was able to learn to read at a third-grade level, is three merit badges away from Eagle Scout, and graduated from high school, and after going through the transition program for youth with special needs, he has become even more independent. Brandon was able to get a real job doing an internship for a large corporation in town and makes ten dollars an hour, doing HR work and takes care of computer files and other office duties. His parents learned that every day with Brandon is a treat. They live with an amazing kid who is hilarious, and they look forward to each day with him. Both of their children are their pride and joy.

> Where is the wise person? Where is the teacher of the law? Where is the philosopher of this age? Has not God make the foolish the wisdom of the world? For since in the wisdom of God the world through its wisdom did not know Him. (1 Corinthians 1:20–21)

> Brothers and sisters, think of what you were when you were called. Not many of you were wise by human standards; not many were influential; not many were of noble birth. But God chose the foolish things of the world to shame the wise; God chose the weak things of the world to shame the strong. God chose the lowly things of this world and the despised things—and the things that are not—to nullify the things that are, so that no one may boast before Him. (1 Corinthians 1:26–29)

I could go on for many more pages with these stories of children that have touched my life and the lives of countless others. The children I've written about are small samples of the miracle kids that I've met in my forty-five-plus years in the world of special education. Each one has added something special to my soul, and I hope I added to theirs. Each child also came with a family that grew to be part of the DLC family.

I think that brings me to the final point of this chapter. Why did I need to fight to keep DLC going? The most important reason to continue fighting for DLC was for the parents and caregivers of these beautiful children. As Rev. Rafe Vigil, one of our past board members and a Methodist minister, said in an interview about DLC, "These parents feel like they are alone on an island, and DLC comes along and rescues them and makes them realize they are not alone after all."

Isn't that why we are all put on this Earth? Some people have been given a harder road to travel, and if we can lighten their load, shouldn't we do it? DLC was created for kids, but I came to realize, over the years, that God intended for DLC to bring hope to the families. Parents of kids with special needs want to see their children learning and happy, no matter how long they live or how much they improve. DLC makes their chaotic, sometimes nightmarish, lives feel like regular lives. Their children come to school and play with other kids and learn as much as they can while the adults get on with jobs and careers. Every day that I can tell a parent something positive about their child, it reminds them that their child is just that—a child! They are not their disability!

I realized, after several years of running DLC, the best part of my day was telling the parents that something wonderful had happened at school. Many of them have struggled to find the joy in parenting a child with so many problems and a child that is medically complex. The children and parents have been through so much, and doctors, sometimes, give them little hope. Rather than focus on a medical condition or handicapping diagnosis and rather than dwell on what their child can't do, DLC would help them look at their sweet little boy or girl and see what they *can* do.

More times than not, children surpass the original expectations that were predicted at the time of diagnosis. Parents have to be made aware of that. Someone needs to tell them their child can overcome that negative prediction. Someone has to support them and inspire them. That's why DLC has to continue! The tagline I thought of the first time I made up a flier to hand out to parents is still true today. DLC is the place "where anything is possible!" And we later added the phrase, "DLC helps your child say, 'Yes, I can!'"

> As He passed by, He saw a blind man since birth. And His disciples asked Him, "Rabbi, who sinned, this man or his parents, that he was born blind?"

> Jesus answered, "It was not that this man sinned, or his parents, but that the works of God might be displayed in him." (John 9:1–3)

But if anyone has the world's goods and sees his brother in need, yet closes his heart against him, how does God's love abide in him? Little children, let us not love in word or talk, but in deed and truth. (1 John 3:17–18)

"For I was hungry and you gave me food, I was thirsty and you gave me drink, I was a stranger and you welcomed me, I was naked and you clothed me, I was sick and you visited me, I was in prison and you came to me."

Then the righteous will answer Him saying, "Lord when did we see You hungry and feed You, or thirsty and we gave You drink? And when did we see You a stranger and welcome You, or naked and clothe You? And when did we see You sick or in prison and visit You?"

Then the King will reply to them, "I assure you when you have done it for one of the least of these brothers or sisters of Mine, you have done it for Me." (Matthew 25:35–46)

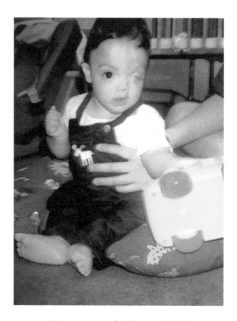

Simon as a baby at DLC

Simon and his mom visiting after he finished 1ˢᵗ grade

Simon's high school graduation picture

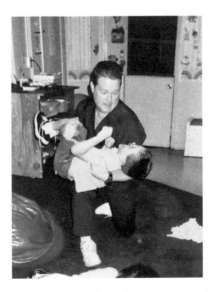

Stephen and Marc wrestling during physical therapy

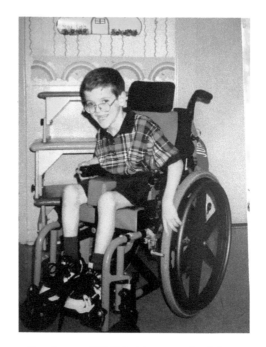

Stephen at DLC is his new wheelchair

Stephen visiting the staff after graduating high
school (Me, Mina, and Mayra)

Brandon and twin sister Brandi around age 3

Brandon's graduation picture and he is so proud

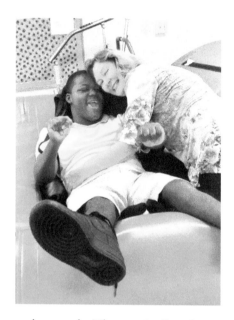

Brandon and me at the Therapy & Care Summer Camp

Baby Andrew with Santa at the DLC Christmas Party

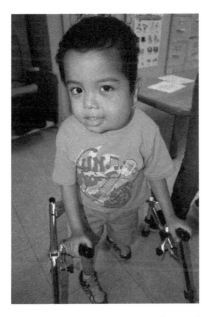

Andrew learning to walk with his walker

Andrew walking independently to get his preschool diploma at DLC

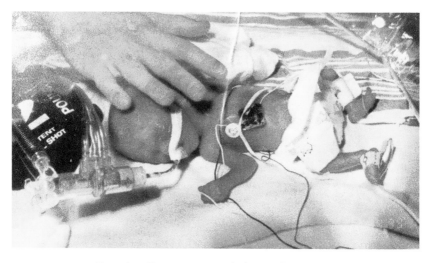

Brandon R as a preemie baby in the NICU

Brandon at home about age 2

Brandon's graduation photo

Brandon as an adult with his family for a photo shoot

# CHAPTER 8

## *Moving Forward*

*"Though the mountains be shaken and the hills be removed, yet My unfailing love for you will not be shaken nor my covenant of peace be removed," says the Lord, who has compassion on you.*

—Isaiah 54:10

Well, as the saying goes, I just decided to "put one foot in front of the other" and just see what happened. No one was shutting us down, and I sure wasn't going to do it. I had the loyal staff left that believed in DLC, and they were willing, along with me, to do whatever it took to keep opening the doors one day at a time.

We put out a heartfelt letter as a plea to the all the United Methodist churches in the North East district. In the letter I included a "church line" I had heard many times from pastors to inspire the congregation to do more outreach in the community. The line goes something like this, "Would anybody notice if we closed our doors, if this church shut down would we be missed?" In my letter, I explained about the families we serve and the many desperate families we would serve in the future. There was no doubt DLC would definitely be missed! I asked each church to take up a collection. The letter showed how each person giving a little could be multiplied by the numbers of each church's membership (thirty members giving ten dollars each multiplied by fifty churches equals fifteen thousand dollars). No amount was too small. If everyone gave a little, it would be big! Well, not every church responded but close to thirty did, and within a few weeks, we raised over eighteen thousand dollars.

The real blessing was that this crisis had awakened a sleeping giant—the church members. It woke up DLC too and our board of directors. We realized that smaller donations were the key to fund-raising that we had been ignoring. We were relying on larger grants that were not always available; but God's people are. The church members had become complacent as DLC grew. The perception was that we didn't need them, and their smaller gifts to DLC weren't needed anymore. Now, they realized we did need them, their prayers, and their donations, no matter how small. And besides, it showed me that the churches really believed in the idea of DLC and still wanted to support us. We had just stopped asking.

> And let us consider each other carefully for
> the purpose of sparking love and good deeds.
> (Hebrews 10:24)

The congregation of believers was one in heart and soul. No one claimed that any of his pos-

sessions was his own, but they shared everything
they owned. (Acts 4:32)

This would not be the last time DLC would have financial trouble, but we always found a way to pull through; rather, God would turn up a resource and pull us through. Each time, I would learn new things, and I definitely learned not to panic. I would almost wait with excitement to see how it would happen this time. It almost became a joke around the staff and a saying came out of it. That phrase became our secret mantra, "You know, everything always works out." We got to where we would say it about all problems—big or small. A day when staff was short due to illness, we would look at each other and say, "It always works out," and less children would show up that day. If we were short on payroll, an unexpected donation would show up in the mail that just covered it. Nonprofit life is definitely living on the edge, and I don't know how others do it if they aren't relying on God.

The summer of 2015 is the best demonstration of God's blessings at the right time. My faith and that DLC mantra would be put to the test. The school year had gone off without a hitch. Our finances seemed in order, and there was a plan in place for administration coverage while I was out for the next few weeks. I was scheduled for major surgery and would miss at least six weeks over the summer months.

The summer months are particularly difficult as staff and the hours they are needed increases. With public schools closed, DLC is needed more than ever. Our students that come after school need full-time care from the beginning of June to mid-August, when school starts up again. Staff payroll increases, as well as supply costs with extra students needing extra snacks, extra cleanup and art supplies, etc. Another financial burden is the cost of utilities during the hot summer in Florida. We prepare for this, but as a nonprofit relying on donations, there is never a perfect financial plan. The budget is more of an educated guess.

The problems, as they usually did, creeped up on us slowly. Many of our donations began to slow down, and several funding sources had changed their system of delivery. This meant grants were going to run out sooner than anticipated. Another grant we were hoping for would not be available until fall. We looked ahead at our funding and realized without, at least, fifty thousand dollars coming from somewhere, we would not be able to remain open the whole summer. This would mean shutting down for July and part of August, until funding started up again for school tuition and annual grants. With me unavailable to do fundraising over the summer, the responsibility would be on my staff to find a way. I put out requests for help to a few of our loyal donors and left for my surgery. All that was left for me to do was pray.

I literally prayed a desperation prayer, with a hint of anger in it, the day I left. I told God it was on Him to get this done! I was not going to panic over this but almost demanded God take over this burden. I remember saying to Him that I have served Him faithfully in my ministry for twenty-six years, and it didn't seem fair to have me upset at a time when I should be taking care of myself. Of course, it was my choice whether or not I was upset, and I suddenly found myself saying, "God you have to take care of DLC, I have to take care of myself this time."

Well, I had my surgery, and the miracles started; several of our funders heard about our difficulty and put a plan together. United Way advanced us $11,000 from our annual funding. The Community Foundation of Northeast Florida brought a funder for a tour, and she donated ten thousand dollars along with another ten thousand dollars from the foundation. Another prominent Jacksonville family donated twenty-five thousand dollars, and through a GoFundMe account set up by my staff, another eight thousand dollars came in. Baptist Health Foundation called a special meeting of their board, and the grant we thought wouldn't be approved until the fall was approved immediately. The funds from Baptist came in by the end of June, giving us the thirty-two thousand dollars we were hoping for.

One of the biggest problems we had faced each year, at summertime, was that our school funding from the Jacksonville Children's Commission ended in June, and the new funding cycle had not ever started until September or after, for the last few years. They were tied into the city funds, and nothing could be done to change the city funding cycle. You can't fight city hall, as the saying goes. But I guess God can! Because of our situation, the funding was moved along more quickly, giving us a forty-thousand-dollar boost by July—three months early. All in all, we ended up with nearly ninety thousand dollars over the fifty thousand dollars we needed for the summer. More than one hundred forty thousand dollars was put in the DLC bank account within a six-week period. I jokingly said that God was just showing off, but He really did!

Not only did this keep us open for the summer but proved to me that DLC can go on without me in the future and that the whole community sees our program as indispensable. So many people and agencies rallied behind us and made sure our doors stayed open; it showed me that I wasn't the only one that saw our program as valuable. I had often felt alone in my fight for this special program to succeed, but now, I knew for certain that I wasn't alone. It does matter to other people that kids with disabilities are cared for and their families have support. People *would* notice if DLC wasn't there! God's plan for DLC to continue matters to many, not just me now! I had my surgery; it was successful, and I was able to relax and heal, knowing my life's work was in good hands.

> And to know the love of Christ that surpasses knowledge, that you may be filled with all the fullness of God. Now to Him who is able to do immeasurably more than all we ask or imagine, according to His power that is at work within us. (Ephesians 3:19–20)

> And God is able to make all grace abound to you, so that in all things, at all times, having all that you need, you will abound in every good work. (2 Corinthians 9:8)

# CHAPTER 9

# *What Is Church, Anyway?*

*This service that you perform is not only supplying the needs of the Lord's people but is also overflowing in many expressions of thanks to God.*

*Because of the services by which you have proved yourselves, others will praise God for the obedience that accompanies your confession of the gospel of Christ and for your generosity in sharing with them and with everyone else. (2 Corinthians 9:12–13)*

I think God's big plan for the church has yet to be fulfilled. I know He loves us to worship on Sunday together. And learning about the Word and how to apply it to our lives is the key to life. But then, what? That leaves the other six days a week to apply it. Isn't that what church is really all about? Real worship is the pouring out of our lives for Him in a sacrificial way.

Now, to be honest, I never thought of that when I started DLC. I really was looking for a way to help some families and kids and support myself while I took care of my children. But I am sure now that God intended it to be much more. I do believe everyone should be finding their Monday-through-Saturday church. And it doesn't need to look like Sunday church. Real spiritual growth happens during service to others.

Helping children with disabilities is an obvious outreach. They are so innocent and need so much. Almost any attempt to help them is worthwhile. And time spent with them is always rewarding. Children with various disabilities come in many different packages, and that doesn't always make things easy when creating a program that supports them. Not only do the children have varying degrees of mental and physical delay, but often, the delays are accompanied by significant medical diagnoses. It is one thing to provide their child care and education needs and quite another to handle the medical care.

Many times, it was questioned why we decided to take on children with medical problems. Wasn't that a big liability risk? That's the way the world thinks, and unfortunately, it's the way many of the church members felt too. So many of them would let the fear of something bad happening prevent all of the good that was happening. This is not of God. If someone is more afraid of a lawsuit, it says they do not think God is big enough to handle the problems.

I saw children and families in need, and they happened to have medical problems. So I looked for a way to take care of them. These were the children no one else wanted to take on. They were the most in need of a place. If we are doing God's work, then, we should be able to trust that He is in control of the work. I don't know how to live my life any other way. Church is not a place to be preserved but used to His glory.

I will try and retell a story that I heard one of the Methodist pastors preach at a business meeting. He was explaining why we can't be afraid of our churches getting dirty and torn up from use. He described a beautiful lighthouse that was in a harbor. It was so beautiful that the town wanted to preserve it and to keep it looking pristine. One night, a large ship started taking on water. The fisherman onboard saw the light house in the distance as they began to sink. The fisherman hoped there was someone in the lighthouse that saw them as they began to sink along with their ship into the sea. The preservation group for the lighthouse considered helping the fisherman and had rescue boats available but decided not to act because if they rescued the men, then, they would have to bring them into the lighthouse. If the fisherman all came into the lighthouse, it would make a big mess with water everywhere, and if the sailors where dirty, then, dirt might get all over the floors and walls. The sailors were probably not the most neat and tidy of people, so they might even do real damage to the lighthouse, and all their hard work restoring the lighthouse could be destroyed. So they let the sailors drown in the sea instead.

Now, this may sound extreme, but it illustrates the need to open our churches for the things that are really needed. There are so many more needs that the church could fulfill but don't because it might be too risky for the church and the congregation. What is more important; people's health and spiritual well-being or having a nice building? Should we welcome children with medical problems into our program or let them sit at home because there might be a lawsuit one day. The answer is obvious, but many times, this situation plays out in reality due to fears church members have over keeping their church building safe.

> For God has not given us a spirit of fear, but of power and love and of a sound mind. (2 Timothy 1:7)

> Remember this: Whoever sows sparingly, will also reap sparingly, and whoever sows generously with reap generously. (2 Corinthians 9:6)

> Now he who supplies seed to the sower and bread for food will also supply and increase your store of seed and will enlarge the harvest of your righteousness. You will be enriched in every way so that you can be generous on every occasion. (2 Corinthians 9:10)

If we are going to be the church, let's really *do* church. What would Jesus do? It may be cliché now but what did He do? I know He reached out to those that others rejected. I know He took risks and wants us to take them as well.

What did Jesus want for the church? I believe the church is our filling station to be filled with the love of God on Sunday so that we can get on with the business of serving and loving others the rest of the week. We are to be adding to the church by demonstrating this love through the church. We all know that church isn't the building; it is the people. Without the people, it is truly an empty shell. If we aren't finding ways to connect to a hurting world through service to them, there will be less and less people to fill that shell and be the church of the future.

Sadly, I see this every year as more and more churches are closing their doors permanently. Could it be that those churches could have done some great service work inside their walls and added to their congregations and become vital again? Churches could be full of people that felt the love through the acts of kindness? Some church buildings are even being sold and bought by other service organizations and nonprofits that are helping the hurting people in our community. I think that is the job of the people of the church. Most of the nonprofits today are secular and don't even talk about God's love to those they are serving. That is the sad truth.

> Be devoted to one another in love. Honor one
> another above yourselves. Never lacking in zeal,
> but keep your spiritual fervor, serving the Lord.
> Be joyful in hope, patient in affliction, faithful
> in prayer. Share with the Lord's people who are
> in need. Practice hospitality. (Romans 12:10–13)

How did Jesus draw people in to Himself? Did He just sit in a building worshipping, reading the scriptures to learn more for Himself? Did Jesus sit in a pew, listening to people teaching and singing psalms and hymns? Did He expect the people to come to Him while he remained in the temple? Of course, He didn't wait on them to realize they needed to come to Him. He went out and got them. He found out who was hurting and loved them and helped them right where they were. He went outside the city gates, to the people that were considered sinners and those considered unworthy; the poor and the hurting and the sick. He often made it a priority to love those that society judged as not acceptable to God. Funny how now we know how wrong they were. God loves those people just as much and many times those judgments were completely wrong. He reaches out to the one lost sheep and leaves the ninety-nine others behind. That is the kind of love that drew them to God. And that is what I hope we are doing with the ministry of DLC. On the surface, it looks like a business that is providing childcare to children with disabilities. But the fact that we are doing special childcare services that others don't provide is key. I think that is why DLC is in a church so people will make that connection. God is loving them through His church so they will be drawn to Him. Judgement pushes people away and loving service pulls them toward.

> And I have other sheep that are not of this fold. I must bring them also, and they will listen to My voice. So there will be one flock, one shepherd. (John 10:16)

> But Christ is faithful over God's house as a son. And we are His house if indeed we hold fast

our confidence and our boasting in our hope.
(Hebrews 3:6)

But be sure to fear the Lord and serve Him faithfully with all your heart; consider what great things He has done for you. (1 Samuel 12:24)

# CHAPTER 10

# *Your Turn*

*To equip the saints for the work of ministry, for the*
*building up of the body of Christ.*

—Ephesians 4:12

God needs so many more willing hearts. Imagine if everyone that loved God and had a relationship with Him decided to do a little bit more? What if everyone that had felt a call or a single nudge to take action did something right away? What if each person that had been blessed by an act of God when they had been in trouble went out and found someone else in trouble to bless? We could change the world. It is possible. After all, with God, anything is possible.

If you are going to be a Christian and say, "I am a Christ Follower," then, really follow Him! How important was it to Jesus to heal the sick, lame, and the poor? The majority of His ministry was spent reaching out to those less fortunate. Once He had their attention and their trust, then, He was able to preach to them. It is the same with us today. Only if we are showing love by helping others can we talk about God's love.

Don't you want to make sure that you share His love with the life you've been given? There is a song on a Christian radio today by a band named For King and Country that asks, "Let my life be the proof of Your love."[1] If you are living a safe life, just going to church and living your life to only take care of yourself and your family, that is not really following Christ. Christ had a ministry, and if you are following His example and are His disciple, then, you must have a ministry too. Start praying about that today. What more is out there for you to do? What skill do you have that can be used in ministry?

> If anyone serves Me, he must follow Me and where I am, there My servant will be also. If anyone serves Me, the Father will honor him. (John 12:26)

> I beseech you therefore, by the mercies of God, that you present your bodies a living sacrifice, holy, acceptable unto God, which is your reasonable service. (Romans 12:1)

> Love one another with brotherly affection. Outdo one another in showing honor. Do not be slothful in zeal, be fervent in spirit; serve the Lord! (Romans 12:10–11)

---

[1] For King and Country song, "The Proof of Your Love."

I am sure it doesn't seem possible. And if you are like I was, you are talking yourself out of it and fast as you thought of something. A million questions are popping up in your head. How do I begin? How can I start something like that now? What in the world could I do that would make a difference? I hope God is prompting you to ask these questions.

There are so many hurting people in the world. Pretty much anywhere you look, there is another sad situation—another worthy cause. The task to serve and fix the world can seem monumental. What can any one person do, and how can someone like you be the answer? After all, you barely have time to keep up with life's demands as it is. I am sure you feel like you are not even doing the best job taking care of the responsibilities you have now.

You may already have something in mind. Actually, God may have already placed an idea in your heart. It may be easy for you to know what to do, with so many needs around you, but hard to take the first step. How can you decide what issue is the one God might have in His plans for you? It's easy to have doubts when fear blocks you from taking action.

One of my biggest inspirations was a leadership speaker I heard in a Christian conference called The Global Leadership Summit. I remember him asking the question, "What is it that makes you angry? What do you think is unjust, unfair, and frustrates you every time you think about it? Like Popeye the Sailor Man, what makes you say, "I can't stands it no more?" Have you thought, *Someone should do something about that, it's just not right?* That is the Holy Spirit moving in your heart and mind to take action.

Many people just push the thought out of their minds. Maybe, it seems too painful or too scary to think about for long. Usually, it just seems too big—too far out of reach! How many times have people quoted the Bible where Jesus proclaims, "The poor will always be with you?" I don't think He meant that as an excuse to do nothing. He was making an entirely different point about His impending death and that it was a good thing for Mary to break the alabaster box and anoint Him with oil. He was close to the end of His time on Earth, and He was being honored. It was an act of love by Mary for the one who had saved her from a terrible life. He couldn't have meant the poor are a waste of time, so don't bother to ever help them.

Besides, starting a ministry or being part of one isn't so you can solve a world problem. You might, but the most important thing is to touch individuals with love. Make a difference so they don't feel all alone. Give them the gift of hope in God.

Someone once asked me, knowing that I had taken a leap of faith when starting DLC, if I thought it was enough to witness to others at your workplace. Was it enough to show others God's love by living a good life? Now, this was a good lady, a very strong Christian, in my humble opinion. My first inclination was to avoid insulting her and grieving her heart. I started to say "yes" and that not everyone is called to have a ministry. But instead, I felt I owed it to her to tell her how I really felt and give her an honest answer. I really don't believe it is enough. This is a world full of hurting and lost people, as well as those that are truly suffering. So many feel so unloved and alone. Besides, I think she wouldn't have asked me if she didn't already feel she was meant to do more.

Could it possibly be okay to simply live our lives, avoid committing one of the major sins, and that be enough? Or is that the biggest sin of all! It can't be enough to know God and His love and do nothing more with your life. Is the sin of omission possibly the one that grieves God the most? If we hold back, it leaves so many others without their needs being met and keeps them from feeling God's love through you. More importantly, it's a shame because people are missing out on the life God had intended for them. A life full of challenges but a life more rewarding than any paycheck could bring.

I don't say these things to make you beat yourself up or insult you but to jump-start you into action. I think there is more for every Christian to experience and more we could all do to turn this world around. To bring more of heaven to Earth! Start praying and looking for the signs; God will show you. Start looking around for your mission in life. As I said earlier, you could already have an idea of what that might be. Maybe, you have known all along, and as you read this book, it kept coming to mind. Whatever the case, I know that there is something you are meant to do. There is too much that needs to be done.

Like Peter, are you just not getting out of the boat? If you don't, you will never really experience Jesus fully and have His assurance that He was the Son of God and not just a good teacher. Are you not putting your net on the other side of your boat? Maybe, you are so stuck in your day-to-day life that you just are afraid to drop your nets, even when you know Jesus is telling you to do it. If that is the case, you may be missing out on the life that would reinvigorate you.

Your biggest blessing might be just around the corner. But you have to turn the corner and stop walking in the same path.

For those that have taken that step out of the boat, I know it wasn't and isn't easy. We need to be encouraged to continue our journey. The blessings are countless, but the challenges are there as well. Even as I write this and reread it, I have felt God encouraging me and reminding me of my calling.

> But when Peter saw the wind, he was afraid and began to sink, and cried out, "Lord, save me!" Immediately Jesus reached out His hand and caught him.
>
> "You of little faith," He said, "why did you doubt?" And when they climbed into the boat, the wind died down. Then those who were in the boat worshipped Him, saying, "Truly You are the Son of God." (Matthew 14:30–32)

> When He finished speaking, He said to Simon, "Put out into the deep water, and let down the nets for a catch."
>
> Simon answered, "Master, we've worked hard all night and haven't caught anything. But because You say so, I will let down my nets." When they had done so, they caught such a large number of fish that their nets began to break. So they signaled their partners in the other boat to

come and help them, and they came and filled both boats so full that they began to sink. When Simon Peter saw this, he fell at Jesus's feet and said, "Go away from me Lord; I am a sinful man!" (Luke 5:4–8)

There may be so much more to your life that you are missing because you are afraid. You may be so close to the biggest haul of your life if you will only listen to the inner voice that is telling you to be obedient and help others in a bigger way—a more risky way than you have been. As I am sure you have guessed the inner voice isn't you; it is the Holy Spirit prompting you to move toward the life He knows is the one He had planned for you since the beginning. It is probably something very near you; maybe, it's just on the other side of *your* boat.

Simon admitted he was a sinful man because he was tired; he had not been successful after trying for a long time, and he really didn't want to do what Jesus told him. After all, he had been fishing all night. Maybe, you have been working hard your whole life, and the thought of adding any other tasks to your agenda is overwhelming. But Peter was obedient and did it anyway.

And the others who came to help Peter pull the fish in filled their boat as well. Is there a ministry that has already caught your attention? God may have plans for you to do something even greater for that ministry that only you can do. You may not be able to start something new. You may be older, not physically able, or not have the time to run a full-time ministry. Only you know if you are like

Peter or the partners that came and helped him bring in all those fish. But no matter who you are or where you are on your journey, being a partner might just be the first step to finding a ministry all you own.

> God has put together all the parts of the body. And He has given more honor to the parts that didn't have any. In that way, the parts of the body will not take sides. All of them take care of one another. If one part is honored every part shares in its joy. You are the body of Christ. Each one of you is a part of it. (1 Corinthians 12:24)

So the first step is to find your ministry, but then, what? Do nothing else until you pray. The last thing you want is to get caught up in a project that was your idea alone. This may be one of the hardest things to decipher. Is it God's will or just your crazy idea? There are no simple answers, which is why I said pray. I can tell you how I decided, but God may show you in a completely different way. I think it is a little like love; you'll know it when it happens.

The way I knew was that all of the events happening around me seemed out of my control and much too obvious to be mere coincidences. This idea just kept coming up in my mind, even in my dream one night. Each time I began to doubt that I could start a ministry, something would happen around me to encourage me. It genuinely felt like God nudged.

There was the lady who donated therapy equipment to me at the right time. Then, later, running into the mother of one of my students in my new neighborhood. These are two examples. Also, the fact that I happened to purchase a home one block from a church, and it was a United Methodist Church like the one in which I was raised. Of course, the most obvious being that we joined and, then, found out the activities director and head pastor both had ties to people with handicaps and special education.

The one thing I will say is that, many times, God wants us to take the first step, and then, the answers will come. If I had never put my idea on the table and risked embarrassment and rejections, then, I might have never found out the information that persuaded me. I would not have ever known that Russ's brothers had been handicapped as children or that Reverend Bill had a mom that was a special-education teacher. If I hadn't taken the leap of faith and left my teaching job, then, I would have never known if a childcare for special kids could really work. That is just something that requires faith and trust in God. Also, and maybe most important is knowing that no matter what, things will work out. Many times, we claim to believe that God is in control and that He loves us. If that is true, then, the only way to give God the chance to prove that to you is to step out in faith.

The worst thing that can happen is that your first attempt fails. But failure is only a stepping-stone. Maybe, the failure will lead you to something else that is even better than your original idea. It may lead you to meet a contact that opens a door to a need you didn't even know existed. It might not be the right time, so God will put off your plans and divert you until the time is right for your idea to be fully realized.

I failed the first two attempts when reaching out to churches but ended up in the one God intended. Every failure along the way taught me something that led to a new success.

There are many things that are exactly as I had envisioned my school would be. But many things are completely different. The drastic difference is the "inclusion" part. That is something that has become the best part of DLC. Students with completely different developmental levels coming together to learn from and play with each other. I never could have imagined that. When I first planned on a childcare, laws had just been passed to ensure all children should be educated in some way by public schools, no matter how severe their disability. Then, the law was passed to educate them in the "least restrictive environment." It wasn't until the mid-'90s that laws addressed this issue, giving children the best opportunity to learn; many times, this meant placing them in a classroom for nondisabled students. This gradually came to mean children shouldn't be separated out and placed in classes with only children that were disabled like they were. And then, it took several years for this law to really take effect. With all of that said, I had no idea, but God did. The fact that we're placing children together from all different levels of development not only helped the children to learn from each other, but it also gave us more income. We could charge them regular childcare prices, and that helped create more scholarship money for the families that really needed it. I think it also gives parents a more positive outlook for their child, and that gives our teachers higher expectations for the children. Even now, DLC is the only school that utilizes inclusion programming as part of its focus. Our goal is a fifty-fifty split of students with and without disabilities in each classroom. Other organizations have a few children that have slight developmental delays, but none do it like DLC.

I certainly didn't consider that my school would have grown into as big a ministry as it has. I saw me and a few children with maybe a couple of staff to help out. I certainly didn't think we would serve over one hundred children each year, be in two locations, and have a staff of thirty. DLC is now considered a major nonprofit program in our city and are shoulder to shoulder with some of the best charitable organizations in Jacksonville. This respect has come to us after less than thirty years of service when most others have been around for close to one hundred years. I have learned if God wants it to happen, it will just happen. But you have to be open and willing to jump when an opportunity comes.

When I come up with a plan—something I think is right for DLC—and then it all just falls into place, then, I know it's from God. Like how our second location worked out! It was the perfect timing for everyone. The church needed us, we needed the space, and the funding was available. But there are times when I thought something was best, and no matter how hard I tried to make it happen, it simply didn't happen. I reached out in faith, and it just didn't happen!

There are times when things just don't line up financially or with a location that, at first, seemed right. You learn to go with the flow.

That flow is God. Then, you know the steps to take or not take. That is how God leads you. He really does lead you every step of the way.

> I will instruct you and teach you in the way you
> should go; I will counsel you with my loving eye
> on you. (Psalm 33:8)

But if you don't step, He can't lead.

The best example of this is from the Indiana Jones movie where they are looking for the chalice of Christ. There is a huge crevasse, and they must cross at a certain point to get to their prize, the chalice from Christ's last supper; but there is no bridge. They figure out from clues that there is something there that can't be seen until they take the first step.

If they are wrong, the consequences will be dire. It appears to their eyes that it is a cliff with a drop off that will mean certain death if they plummet to the bottom. As soon as Indiana puts his foot down and shifts his weight forward, the bridge appears. That scene meant so much to me because that was my story. I had to take that first blind step and leave my teaching job to start the school. Things became clearer with each step I took. Indiana made it across on the bridge that became visible to him, and I did too.[2]

Maybe, none of this makes sense to you now, but I think it will if you start thinking seriously about God's plan for your life and a ministry that might be the one for you. I know it also does not sound easy. There were many ups and downs in my ministry, even though I

---

[2]  Indiana Jones movie, "The Last Crusade."

truly believe God was in it and guiding me. That is really the point; it isn't supposed to be easy. Life isn't supposed to be easy. What do you think we are on Earth to do? I'm sure you have wondered why God put us here in the first place. I doubt He sent us here to realize there is a God so we could just go to church and hang out. I don't think He sent us down here to party and lounge around with nothing but blessings happening around us every day. I think that sounds more like heaven than Earth. God knows what is best for His children, just as we know what is better for our children when they are young and inexperienced, as well. He is our Father helping us to mature spiritually as we help our own kids as they grow and mature.

I think we are here for a reason, and I know I said that before; we are here to be in ministry to others. But I'm not repeating myself. I mean, there is an ultimate reason we are here that answers the ultimate question. What is the point of all of this? What is the meaning of life for all of us. It's not about the ministry and making it successful. Of course, we are here to find our calling and eventually do something that helps others and to share the love we have received from God. But ultimately, it is about learning all we need to learn while we are here. That doesn't happen when things are going perfectly.

When my ministry is successful, I feel like I have accomplished what God sent me here to do. But really, it's been about the journey and the struggles and, yes, more about the failures than the successes. The times of failure were when I was learning to rely on God and trust that He has me in the palm of His hand. It is also when I learned about myself and how to become a better person. When I was struggling is when the real-life lessons were being taught. I have known, and you probably know this too, that the real valuable times in life are when life is hard. That is really when you know you are choosing what God wants you to do. If something is hard, it's worth doing. It might be hard but still is something you can accomplish, just something that takes real effort and discomfort. It will also be something you can't accomplish on your own. You will need God and others to make it happen. Don't be afraid of a challenge; look forward to the lessons you will learn in the challenge. And look for God in the middle of the challenges. That is when you will learn that God *is* real, His Word *is* alive, and He really does love you and will take care of you.

It is also when you will receive the real blessings in life. Riches and buying things give us security and temporary happiness, but the real blessings can be felt in our hearts and in our souls. These are the blessings we receive from giving others comfort and joy. The blessing of living a life that is a blessing to others and feeling a sense of accomplishment that is unlike any other. It is all too often we see those that have reached the top financially, but they get there and feel all alone. How many wildly successful people end up depressed, living out-of-control lives, on drugs, or worse, committing suicide. Nothing feels better than a life well lived; one that pleases God and brings real and permanent joy.

> But seek ye first the kingdom of God and His
> righteousness and all these things will be given to
> you as well. (Matthew 6:33)

The other advice I have is to take the step to get started but a small step. And I don't mean a timid first step. I only mean don't bite off more than you can chew. If you do what you can do on your own, then, God will start filling in the rest. So give God that opportunity. Take a step and, then, wait, listen, and learn. Here is an example of what I am suggesting, and this is how DLC started. I didn't open the doors at two locations with ten classrooms and hire thirty staff and enroll eighty children. I did some research and found out there was a need, enrolled a few children, and then, waited to see how it would go. As I saw the needs and God showed me things that were missing, I, then, filled in gaps. When more students wanted to attend, I hired more staff. When families needed help with tuition, I started the scholarship fund. When children with medical problems wanted to enroll, we found a volunteer nurse. I think all of these things were promptings from God as He was designing the way DLC would change and grow. It was also the best way for me to change and grow along with the ministry.

As the program was growing, I was learning, little by little, what I needed to know. Also, I was growing spiritually in my faith and trust.

The most important thing of all is to remember God is in control and you are not.

This is His ministry being carried out through one of His servants. You are the servant and don't think of yourself as anything more. Never get too carried away with the importance of the ministry or yourself. God will have a way of slowing you down, and He knows how to humble you very quickly. And when you are humbled by God, you are really humbled.

The most important lesson is to remember to go to Him in prayer and don't try and figure everything out by yourself. For one thing, you can't figure everything out, and you will go crazy trying.

Pray and wait and listen, and the answer will come. It will come through others, through His Word, or just through a solution that presents itself suddenly and unexpectedly. Those are the wow God moments! Those are the times that knock your socks off and make you know without a shadow of a doubt that God is God. After this happens a few times, you will learn to expect it, and that is where God wants you to be. Then, He can really use you. That is when you will truly enjoy the life you were intended to have.

> For the Lord corrects those He loves, just as a father disciplines a child in whom he delights. (Proverbs 3:12)

> My child, do not make light of the Lord's discipline. And do not lose heart when He rebukes you, because the Lord disciplines the one He loves, and He chastens everyone He accepts as His child. Endure hardship as discipline; God is treating you as His children. For what children are not disciplined by their father? (Hebrews 12:5–7)

There is an old song by Stephen Curtis Chapman that explains this point so well.

He says, "I opened up the Bible and read about me." This really tells how the Bible really becomes "your Bible," when you are stepping out in faith. He goes on to say, "Saddle up your horses, we've got a trail to blaze. Through the wild blue yonder of God's amazing grace. Let's follow our leader into the glorious unknown. This is life like no other. This is the great adventure!"[3] As you can see, I found God's guidance in many different places. I was living the lyrics of songs I heard on the radio. When something touches you in your soul, then, you know it is a prompting from God!

Do you want to live the life of the great adventure, full of its lessons and blessings and fullness? Then, don't hold back! Don't let fear steal the most exciting and joyous life from you that you could have—the one God has preordained for you. Fear is the devil's tool to take away the joy in which your life can be filled. Just get started by taking that first step into the unknown. Know you are not the first, and others have taken similar risks like me and many others before me. Many others have taken bigger leaps in more risky ways. Get started on the first chapter in your book. The book of your real-life story. The one God started writing before you were born.

> Therefore I tell you, do not worry about your life, what you will eat or drink; what you will wear. Is not life more than food, and the body more than clothes? Look at the birds of the air; they do not sow or reap or store away in barns, and yet your heavenly Father feeds them. Are you not much more valuable than they? (Matthew 6:25–26)

---

[3] Steven Curtis Chapman song, "The Great Adventure."

# CHAPTER 11

## *Never-Ending Story*

*And I am sure of this, the He who began a good work in you will bring it to completion at the day of Jesus*

—Christ. Philippians 1:6

I really wanted a nice and tidy ending to the story; some big, huge achievement that had happened to the program before I finished the book. I always thought some millionaire would hear about DLC and what we are doing and give us the money to build a huge facility or multiple facilities. I thought by the time I was ready to publish, we might start DLC programs all over Florida or the country. But that hasn't happened yet. I still hope it will, and I really believe it will one day. It might happen now that I have retired or even after I have died, and I will watch it from heaven.

Of course, the real big accomplishment is just DLC, itself, all the children that have come and gone and become independent, happy, and successful adults. The fact that parents were helped and given the support to have careers and were able to keep their families together and made them stronger. The fact that staff and volunteers got to be a part of this wonderful experience and absorb the love and joy that the special children around them gave off. There have been so many of the youth and volunteers who went on to become great teachers, nurses, and therapists themselves. Even if one child or adult felt the love of God through DLC and realized God was with them, then, it would have been all worth it.

The real mind-blowing accomplishment, in my opinion, is the fact that with my lack of business education and management skills, we were able to keep it going while other businesses shut down or went into bankruptcy, even big businesses. At the time of this book, DLC has now celebrated its thirtieth year of existence. That is proof that truly anything is possible.

I am tired but happy, and I gradually trained staff to take over from me. We have gone from me having all the responsibility from open to close each day, to multiple staff taking over the many aspects of running a nonprofit. We now have a head nurse, who works at our second location as well—DLC Therapy & Care. The nurse oversees multiple certified nursing assistants and staff at both locations. We had a program director, Miss Mayra, at our original location, who has recently retired after being with DLC for over twenty-two years. Mayra trained two assistant directors, and one has now taken over and oversees the teaching staff, as well as all licensing requirements. We have certified teachers in every classroom with teaching assistants for each of them. Also, there are head teachers at both locations. There is a full-time occupational therapist, Miss Carol, who is the director of therapy services. Carol has been with DLC nearly twenty years and has helped write grants and secured other funding to help families afford therapy and other services. There is a part-time speech therapist, physical therapist, and physical therapist assistant. There is a full-time administrative director that runs the office and an administrative assistant that does public relations and fundraising. We have recently hired a licensed special-education teacher to run the education portion and curriculum for the programs. She assists teachers in all the classrooms to help assure children reach their full potential and does one-on-one tutoring for students that really need it to succeed. All of this would have been mind-blowing to me in the beginning but, now, is just part of the ministry and has been built around specific needs of the children and families we serve. Each role is vital to daily operations, and I am hoping for financial security of DLC well into the future.

> Do not despise these small beginnings, for the Lord rejoices to see the work begin, to see the plumb line in Zerubbabel's hand. (Zechariah 4:10)

> It will be like a man going on a journey, who call his servants and entrusted them with his wealth. To one he gave five bags of gold, to another two bags and to another one bag, each according to his ability. Then he went on his journey.
>
> The man who had received five bags of gold went at once and put his money to work and gained five more bags. Also the one with two

bags of gold gained two more. But the man who had received one bag went off, dug a hole in the ground and buried his master's money. After a long time the master of those servants returned and settled accounts with them.

The man who had received five bags of gold brought the other five. "Master," he said, "you have entrusted me with five bags of gold and I have gained five more."

His master replied, "Well done good and faithful servant. You have been faithful in a few things, I will put you in charge of many things. Come and share in your master's happiness!"

The man with two bags of gold also came. "Master," he said, "you entrusted me with two bags of gold; see, I have gained two more."

His master replied, "Well done, good and faithful servant! You have been faithful with a few things; I will put you in charge of many things. Come and share in your master's happiness!"

The man who had received one bag of gold came, "Master," he said, "I knew you were a hard man, harvesting where you have not sown and gathering where you have not scattered seed. So I was afraid and went out and hid your gold in the ground. See, here is what belongs to you."

His master replied, "You wicked, lazy servant! So you knew that I harvest where I have not sown and gather where I have not scattered seed? Well then, you should have put my money on deposit with the bankers, so that when I returned I would have received it back with interest. So take the bag of gold from him and give it to the one who has ten bags. For whoever has will be given more, and they will have an abundance. Whoever does not have, even what they have will be taken from them." (Matthew 25:14–29)

This is a long scripture but such an important one. We all notice that those who did something with their gift gained more and pleased the master. But do you notice that the one who hid his gift did it because he saw the master as hard. He was afraid of what might happen if he risked it. He also saw the master as unfair, taking what didn't belong to him. I'm sure all children feel that way about their parents.

All of these misconceptions of God exist today. He is not the God of punishment when we, in earnest, are trying our best. God looks on the heart. He knows your intentions. If you are putting forth your best effort with a pure intention, you will be rewarded. If you hold back, live your life out of fear of failure, then and only then do you need to fear God. He will only be disappointed if He has given you this gift of life and blessings, and you hide them and waste your time on Earth. If you have been given more than others,

He expects even more. How long will He wait for you to invest your life into His kingdom. How long will He wait for you to realize there is more, giving you time to take the first step and put your gifts to work. I can't wait to hear God say, "Well done, you good and faithful servant. Come share in your master's happiness!" And I want to share in that happiness with more people. I want you to hear those words too.

> Therefore, since we have received a kingdom that cannot be shaken, let us show gratitude, by which we may offer to God an acceptable service with reverence and awe. (Hebrews 12:28–29)

What I want more than anything is for more people to start paying attention to God's still small voice. I have realized through my journey that God is intervening in our lives all the time. Maybe because of the great needs I experienced during the running of the ministry, I had to rely on Him more. If you start looking for God in your life, you will see Him. Every event, person, Bible verse, and idea that comes your way may be a whisper from the Divine. Get in the habit of looking for God in everything. Especially when you need to make an important decision. The other time to listen extra hard is when you have made a mistake. He will always show you how to correct it and how to do it better the next time. God is alive, and He is the God of the living. Don't wait until you get to heaven to start looking for Him. You need Him much more right now.

I remain confident of this: I will see the goodness of the Lord in the land of the living. (Psalm 27:13)

Hear my voice when I call, Lord and be merciful to me. My heart says of you, "Seek His face!" Your face Lord, I will seek. Do not hide Your face from me. (Psalms 27:7–8)

I hope this is getting you excited about serving God in a bigger way. I don't want to condemn and guilt anyone into a life they may not be ready for. God's timing is more important than a book you read. The point of the book is to get you pumped up. I want to turn you on to a life you might have missed, otherwise.

I pray that the eyes of your heart may be enlightened in order that you may know the hope to which He has called you, the riches of His glorious inheritance in His holy people. (Ephesians 1:18)

If you love God with all your heart, I believe you want to go deeper into a relationship with Him. You want to be sure He is there and that He really loves you. You want to know that God is totally in control. In control not only of your life but of everyone's lives. If you step out in faith to serve Him in a way that tests your faith by doing exactly what you know He wants you to do, then, you will know Him. You will find a God like you never really knew existed before.

You will become very well-acquainted with the God of the universe. Through serving Him more fully, your doubts will be erased by seeing His power in your life over and over again. God is the god of your childhood, the one everyone taught you about in Sunday school. But sadly, so many people go through life, never meeting Him up close. They still think of God as the old man with a beard in the sky that is too far away, too lofty to touch. Or they see God as the angry overseer of the universe, waiting for them to make a mistake so He can punish them. He is none of that, but you have to find out who He really is for yourself. He is the loving, guiding Father of your soul that wants to give you and everyone around you a fulfilled life. This book is meant to introduce you to Him and help you find your path to the joy of serving his people.

I hope through my story of how I learned to count on God, you will be inspired to listen more closely. You will now know to be more aware of thoughts, which may be hints from God. These thoughts may be God nudging you into action. Don't just think about ways you can make a difference; start making a difference. These ideas are hints that God has already been giving you. I hope you won't ignore the longing in your soul for a more meaningful life and the pain you feel over situations of suffering you see. There may also be a feeling of guilt for not doing more to help.

God didn't put pain and guilt in our hearts to just make us feel bad about things we see. That pain is the tool He uses to spur us on to be people of God that do works in His name. We are His hands and feet; we are His love on Earth. If we have experienced His love and have given our lives over to Him, let's make our time here mean something. God's love becomes real to others through us and is multiplied over and over with each person with which we are able to share it. If you love God and know His love is real, then, prove it. I dare you!

I know I have proven it to myself. His love is real, and I can see the power of His love through the day-to-day operations of DLC. This school could not have happened nor been maintained all these years without the awesome power of God. There have been so many stories of the miracles that have happened over the years, and I have shared some of them with you in this book. I also know there will be many more. There have been kid miracles, financial miracles, miracles with the parents we have served and with the volunteers. This book contains an amazing story because our God is an amazing God, and He will give you an amazing life if you let Him. I finally get to tell everyone what He has done. I can't wait to hear from those that read this story of God in action and discover the things God will do for them. The best way to find Him is by living your life doing things for Him, which is doing things for others. When you do, God is actually working through you. I believe there is nothing more amazing than that being your life's legacy.

> In that day you will say: Give praise to the Lord, proclaim His name; make known among the nations what He has done, and proclaim that His name is exalted. Sing to the Lord, for He has done glorious things; let His name be known to all the world. Shout aloud and sing for joy, peo-

ple of Zion, for great is the Holy One of Israel among you. (Isaiah 12:4–6)

Some went out on ships; they were merchants on the mighty waters. They saw the works of the Lord, His wonderful deeds in the deep. (Psalms 107:23–24)

# My Little Angel

# By Alice Taylor with John Pyatt

I write this story to help other parents who might ever go through the same situation.

My story starts June 5, 1964. My husband and I were expecting our third child. Our first two girls—Tammie, five, and Tracy, two—were born healthy and without any problems. Since we had two girls, we were so hoping for a boy as most parents would with two girls in the family. If I had known then what I know now, I wouldn't have hoped so much for a boy but only for another happy, healthy baby.

I received the news on the day I was leaving the hospital with my baby girl. She was no smaller than any other newborn baby and looked no different to me, but when the doctors and nurses all converged on me, I knew something was wrong. I was alone in my room, waiting for check out time when the pediatrician told me my child had brain damage and would never be normal. He described her as "mongoloid." We now know this as Down syndrome. He said she would be behind other children by many years in her growth and her mentality. He went on to tell me she would never be able to walk or talk and would probably never be able to join in the family life at all.

At that time, I really didn't know what he was saying to me. However, I did understand one thing—he wanted me to sign a paper to put her in an institution. I knew I could never give her up no matter what he said! I also thought he was wrong about her. Then he told me I needed to leave her in the hospital for a few days, but I refused. I left that day with my precious new baby in spite of the doctor's advice.

Driving home with my husband sitting beside me, holding my little Tina in my arms, I decided I could never give her up. She was so tiny and helpless, and I knew she needed me just as much or more than my other children. My husband was so wonderful and understanding. He didn't want to give her up either.

I didn't tell anyone, except our families about Tina's diagnosis, not because we were ashamed of her but because I still thought the doctors were wrong. Tina was a good baby and seldom cried. I still didn't believe there was anything wrong with her. When the time came for Tina's first checkup, I took her to the doctor that first told me about her situation. He again tried to get me to put her in an institution. He said she would be better off there since keeping her would be very harmful to my other two children. He went on to tell me I would have to give too much attention to Tina, which would cause my other two girls to be neglected, and they would become jealous of her. Again, I held my resolve and refused to sign her over to him. It always got me upset to talk to this pediatrician. It infuriated me that he continued to insist I put her in a home.

I then decided to get a second opinion about her condition and took her to another pediatrician. I just couldn't make myself believe that the first doctor was right about my baby. All the statistics say that it's very unusual for someone my age to have a baby with Down syndrome. It most often happens to older women or very young girls, and I was only twenty-three, and my husband was twenty-five. It just didn't make sense.

I took Tina to Dr. Skinner, a very wonderful pediatrician who was well known in my town of Jacksonville, Florida. I was so afraid and didn't know what to expect, so two of my sisters went with me. Dr. Skinner examined her very carefully, and he turned to tell me that the first doctors had been right. Tina did have Down syndrome. He went on to explain to me how she was different to help me understand. He showed me she had low muscle tone in her legs and also in the rest of her body. Her eyes were slightly slanted, and she had short fingers and a thick neck. These were things that you just wouldn't notice or maybe I had refused to notice. He also explained that she would be very susceptible to contracting illnesses and get sick easily. He said she had a very mild case, but that when she reached one year of age, her appearance would change a great deal. At that time, I would be able to see that she was developing differently than other children. But then he told me something that relieved me greatly. He said an institution was no place for Tina. She would be a wonderful, loving baby and would eventually be able to walk and to talk. She would just be a few years behind other children her age. This doctor advised us to treat her just like our other girls, even with discipline, and she would learn. He said we could take her to as many doctors as we wanted to, but we would still get the same answer.

I finally realized the truth about Tina. I had faith in Dr. Skinner, so I decided he would always be Tina's pediatrician. My husband and I had to face the facts. She was different and would always be different. But now we had hope, thanks to this caring doctor. When I told my husband the things Dr. Skinner had explained to me, we talked over all the difficulties we would have to face in keeping her. We realized all the attention she would require for many years. Yet we were willing to do anything it took to keep our daughter. Our other two children were old enough and had received my attention when they were babies. Now I felt Tina should have her share. Also, they could be a great help giving her the love she would need.

We went on with our lives as normally as possible. I no longer tried to keep Tina's problem a secret. There was no reason to be ashamed. I loved her no matter what happened. Not knowing very much about her condition, I read everything I could find about it. I was still hoping that she would be much better than the doctors had predicted. All the information I read confirmed my belief that Tina was not as severe a case as others. She still didn't match the descriptions.

When Tina reached six months of age, I began seeing that she, in fact, was different. She wasn't able to sit up or hold her head up like other babies were doing at that age. It would always hurt each time I noticed the differences, but I hid my sadness. I kept the hope alive that she would walk and talk one day, even if it came slowly.

It seemed she always had a cold, so I was extra careful with her. No matter how hard I tried, she would end up back at the doctor's office with another bad cold. Nevertheless, she brought great joy to our home. She was always happy, and a word from her sisters would bring a big smile. When they were away, she really seemed to miss them. They always played with her so well, and she learned to expect it.

There was no great change in her appearance like we had anticipated although she was still very small for a one year old. We never showed her any partiality. She got her share of "nos" and spankings on the hand when she touched something she shouldn't. It always hurt me to fuss at her, but I knew she needed to learn right from wrong. She always understood when she had done something she shouldn't. She hated it when her sisters got in trouble even more, and when they cried, she cried along with them. That showed me her love for us had grown along with our love for her.

After Tina's second birthday, she was rushed to the hospital with pneumonia. I'm afraid I went all to pieces. The doctor had warned us to expect illnesses often, but it didn't make it any easier. We had known this would happen sometime and would probably happen many more times in the future. I also knew I could not let myself become so emotional every time she became ill.

She stayed in the hospital four days. I was with her every minute of her stay. The doctor had her under an oxygen tent the first day to help her breath, and the other three days, she just had to have a vaporizer. She looked so tiny under that big tent it broke my heart. I was sure she thought I didn't love her anymore because I couldn't hold her. Every time I left the room, she cried for me. It hurt so much for her to hold her little arms out for me to take her knowing I couldn't. I usually cried along with Tina. The good thing was, there was always someone in the room talking to her or playing with her. Everyone in the hospital fell in love with her. We all were relieved when the doctor said Tina could finally come home, and she was so happy to see her sisters again.

After Tina's stay in the hospital, she seemed to do things so much better. She was still very small for her age, as she weighed only seventeen and a half pounds. She never seemed to gain weight regardless of how much she ate. She always looked chubby, but I still worried about her not gaining weight. The doctor explained to me that it was normal for her, but I couldn't help worrying.

Soon after that, she started pulling up, crawling, and saying a few words. She is always very loving and such a joy to have around. A day doesn't go by that she doesn't put her little arms around each of us and give us a big hug and kiss. She has finally started taking steps by herself. Her every accomplishment is a thrill to everyone, including her. Every day is something new for Tina and her family. She is always learning new things. Her favorite playmate is Tracy because she treats Tina like a friend and not a baby. Tammie, at the age of seven, tries hard to be like a mother to her. She always holds her and pats her like a baby. But Tina doesn't want to be held anymore because she thinks she is a big girl and wants to be on the move.

Tina loves her grandmother dearly. Although she sees her almost every day, she always squeals and laughs with joy every time she sees Gran open the door. Tina loves music and always dances when she hears the Beatles or Elvis on the radio. She usually tries to stand and dance with her sisters but isn't balanced enough yet. This usually ends with her losing her balance and falling down. She isn't upset by this. She just sits and claps her little hands, wanting us to clap for her too, which, of course, we all do!

We don't know what the future holds for Tina, and we try hard not to think that far ahead. In our hearts, we know we have done the right thing in keeping our baby. I have often thought about the first pediatrician who advised me to give her up, and I can only thank God in helping us make the right decision. In a small way, I pray we have brought as much joy into Tina's life as she has to ours. I only hope reading this will help other parents who might have to make this big decision for I can see no greater joy in life than keeping and loving my little angel.

*Sadly, Tina did not live much past her fourth birthday. Aunt Alice and Uncle Johnny wanted me to share this story along with my own. She and they were the inspiration that I believe guided my life's work. Much in our society has changed in the accepting of individuals with developmental differences but, unfortunately, not enough. The main problem is still a lack of services and funding to support families when children are brought home. I hope, along with all families, that things will change faster but only if we all care and get involved.*

# DLC Nurse & Learn Information

You too can help take care of the angels at DLC! To support the children at DLC Nurse & Learn and DLC Therapy & Care please donate on the DLC Website—www.dlcnl.org or mail to 4101-1 College Street, Jacksonville, Florida, 32205. Donations can be made to the Amy Buggle Scholarship Fund to assist low income families cover the cost of tuition, nursing care and therapy services. Your donation is fully tax deductible and will let families know they are not alone.

This is the original DLC logo

# ABOUT THE AUTHOR

Amy Buggle is the founder of DLC Nurse & Learn, a not-for-profit childcare center that serves children with disabilities and medical complications. DLC's two locations now provide year-round education, nursing care, and therapies to children of all abilities, giving them and their families the opportunity to reach their maximum potential.

Amy Buggle received her bachelor's degree in special education from the University of Florida, was a Duval County schoolteacher for four years, and was elected Teacher of the Year at Mt. Herman School in 1989. Amy has worked professionally in the field of special education since 1985, after volunteering with special-needs children since the age of ten. She was the executive director of DLC Nurse &

Learn for thirty years and, before retiring in January of 2020, was a Sherwood Smith Award winner in 2012 for her work with children, Eve Award finalist in Education in 2013, and a finalist in 2014 for the Mayor's Commission on the Status of Women, Women's History Award for women who have made a difference in Jacksonville, Florida. Amy continues to advocate for children with disabilities and their families through her board membership at the Early Learning Coalition of Duval and in the NE Florida community, as well as serve DLC in an advisory capacity.

CPSIA information can be obtained
at www.ICGtesting.com
Printed in the USA
JSHW052040220321
12801JS00004B/4